2021

HANDBOOK OF
STATISTICS

UNITED NATIONS

Geneva, 2021

Requests to reproduce excerpts or to photocopy should be addressed to the Copyright Clearance Center at copyright.com.

All other queries on rights and licences, including subsidiary rights, should be addressed to:

United Nations Publications
405 East 42nd Street
New York, New York 10017
United States of America
Email: publications@un.org
Website: shop.un.org

The designations employed and the presentation of material on any map in this work do not imply the expression of any opinion whatsoever on the part of the United Nations concerning the legal status of any country, territory, city or area or of its authorities, or concerning the delimitation of its frontiers or boundaries.

A dispute exists between the Governments of Argentina and the United Kingdom of Great Britain and Northern Ireland concerning sovereignty over the Falkland Islands (Malvinas). The final boundary between the Sudan and the South Sudan has not yet been determined. The final status of the following territories has not yet been agreed or determined: Abyei area, Aksai Chin, Arunachal Pradesh, Bi'r Tawil, Hala'ib Triangle, Ilemi Triangle, Jammu and Kashmir, Kuril Islands, Paracel Islands, Scarborough Shoal, Senkaku Islands, Spratly Islands.

The publication has not been formally edited.

United Nations publication issued by the United Nations Conference on Trade and Development.

TD/STAT. 46

ISBN: 978-92-1-112997-7
eISBN: 978-92-1-001061-0
ISSN: 1992-8408
eISSN: 2225-3270
Sales No.: E.22.II.D.2

Notes

The tables in this handbook represent extractions from or analytical summaries of datasets contained in the UNCTADstat Data Center, available at:

https://unctadstat.unctad.org/

UNCTADstat is continuously updated and enhanced, thus providing users with the latest available data. Consequently, the figures from this handbook, which presents statistics at a point in time, may not always correspond with the latest figures in UNCTADstat.

Basic information on concepts, definitions and calculation methods of the presented data are provided in the boxes titled "Concepts and definitions" in each section and in annex 6.3 of this handbook. More detailed information on the sources and methods used for production of data available in UNCTADstat can be found in the documentation attached to the respective UNCTADstat dataset (UNCTAD, 2021a).

Where the designation "economy" appears, it refers to a country, territory or area. The assignment of economies to specific groups is done for statistical convenience and does not imply any assumption regarding the political or other affiliation of these economies by the United Nations. Likewise, the designations "developing" and "developed" are intended for statistical convenience and do not necessarily express a judgement about the stage reached by a particular economy in the development process.

Due to the removal of the "transition economies" group, the classification of economies into "developing" and "developed" applied in this handbook is different from the classification used in previous editions. Also, a broader definition of small island developing States (SIDS) is applied, as defined by the United Nations Office of the High Representative for the Least Developed Countries, Landlocked Developing Countries and the Small Island Developing States (UN-OHRLLS). The corresponding group aggregates are therefore not comparable with data presented in previous handbooks. For more details, see annex 6.2 of this handbook.

Unless otherwise specified, the values of groups of economies represent the sums of the values of the individual economies included in the group. Calculation of these aggregates may take into account data estimated by the UNCTAD secretariat that are not necessarily reported separately. When data coverage is insufficient within a group of economies, no aggregation is undertaken and the symbol (-) is assigned.

Due to rounding, values do not necessarily add up exactly to their corresponding totals.

United States dollars (US$) are expressed in current United States dollars of the year to which they refer, unless otherwise specified. "Ton" means metric ton (1 000 kg).

Due to space constraints, the names of the following countries may appear in abbreviated form: the Plurinational State of Bolivia, the Democratic People's Republic of Korea, the Democratic Republic of the Congo, the Islamic Republic of Iran, Lao People's Democratic Republic, the Federated States of Micronesia, the United Kingdom of Great Britain and Northern Ireland, and the Bolivarian Republic of Venezuela.

The UNCTAD Handbook of Statistics 2021 is available in PDF format from the UNCTAD website, at:
https://unctad.org/HandbookOfStatistics.

The world by development status

Developing economies
Developed economies
/// Least developed countries (LDCs)

The boundaries and names shown and the designations used on this map do not imply official endorsement or acceptance by the United Nations.

2021

Handbook
of Statistics

TABLE OF **CONTENTS**

List of maps and figures

List of tables

Introduction

The UNCTAD Handbook of Statistics 2021 provides a wide range of statistics and indicators relevant to the analysis of international trade, investment, maritime transport and development. Reliable statistical information is indispensable for formulating sound policies and recommendations that may commit countries for many years as they strive to integrate into the world economy and improve the living standards of their citizens.

The UNCTAD Handbook of Statistics and the UNCTADstat Data Center make internationally comparable sets of data available to policymakers, research specialists, academics, officials from national governments, representatives of international organizations, journalists, executive managers and members of non-governmental organizations. In addition, these statistics underpin all UNCTAD activities. Whether for research, policy advice or technical cooperation, UNCTAD needs reliable and internationally comparable trade, financial and macroeconomic data, covering several decades and for as many countries as possible.

This year's online edition again incorporates interactive charts and maps. The choropleth maps help to make smaller territories more visible. We encourage users to explore these features using the online version of the handbook or e-handbook available at: https://stats.unctad.org/handbook/. The e-handbook is a fully interactive tool, including maps and charts, that allow readers to directly access the data from the UNCTADstat Data Center associated with each table or chart.

With the release of 2020 data, the impacts of the COVID-19 pandemic are evident in a myriad of indicators in this 2021 edition. The handbook accordingly provides a wide overview of the consequences of the pandemic across a variety of sectors. As in previous editions, several nowcasts for the current year are included. Given the increased importance of timely data, the handbook has been supplemented by quarterly trade nowcasts, see also:

https://unctad.org/MerchandiseTradeNowcast.

Abbreviations and Symbols

Abbreviations

BPM6	Balance of Payments and International Investment Position Manual, Sixth Edition
BRICS	Brazil, Russia, India, China and South Africa
CIF	cost, insurance and freight
CPI	consumer price index
Dem. Rep.	Democratic Republic
dwt	dead-weight tons
EBOPS 2010	2010 Extended Balance of Payments Services Classification
FDI	foreign direct investment
FOB	free on board
G20	Group of Twenty
GDP	gross domestic product
gt	gross tons
HIPCs	heavily indebted poor countries
HS	Harmonized Commodity Description and Coding System
IMF	International Monetary Fund
ISIC	International Standard Industrial Classification of All Economic Activities
ITC	International Trade Centre
LDCs	least developed countries
LLDCs	landlocked developing countries
LNG	liquefied natural gas
LPG	liquefied petroleum gas
LSBCI	liner shipping bilateral connectivity index
LSCI	liner shipping connectivity index
Rep.	Republic
SAR	Special Administrative Region
SIDS	small island developing States
SITC	Standard International Trade Classification
TEU	twenty-foot equivalent unit
UCPI	UNCTAD Commodity Price Index
UN-OHRLLS	United Nations Office of the High Representative for the Least Developed Countries, Landlocked Developing Countries and the Small Island Developing States
UNSD	United Nations Statistics Division
US$	United States dollars
WTO	World Trade Organization

Symbols

0   Zero means that the amount is nil or negligible.

_   The symbol underscore indicates that the item is not applicable.

..   Two dots indicate that the data are not available or are not separately reported.

-        The use of a hyphen on data area means that data is estimated and included in the aggregations but not published.

A en dash between years (e.g. "1985–1990") signifies the full period involved, including the initial and final years.

(e)   Estimated data

(u)   Preliminary estimate

1

International merchandise trade

KEY FIGURES **2020**

Value of
world merchandise
exports
US$17.6 trillion

Change of
world merchandise
exports
-7.4%

LDCs' share in
global exports
1.03%

NOWCAST **2021**

Growth of global
merchandise exports
+22.4%

1.1 Total merchandise trade

Map 1.1 | **Merchandise exports as a ratio to gross domestic product, 2020**
(Percentage)

- 50 and more
- 30 to less than 50
- 20 to less than 30
- 10 to less than 20
- 0 to less than 10
- No data

Concepts and definitions

The figures on international merchandise trade in this chapter measure the value of goods which add or subtract from the stock of material resources of an economy by entering or leaving its territory (United Nations, 2011). This definition is slightly different from the definition of trade in goods in the balance-of-payments framework (see section 3.2).

The value of exports is mostly recorded as the free-on-board (FOB) value, whereas the value of imports includes cost (for clearance), insurance and freight (CIF).

The trade balance is calculated as the difference between the values of exports and imports.

Merchandise trade figures from 2014 to 2020, at total product level with partner world, are jointly produced by UNCTAD and the World Trade Organization (WTO).

Seasonal adjustments are based on UNCTAD secretariat calculations using X-13ARIMA-SEATS.

Decline in 2020, strong recovery in 2021

In 2020, the value of world merchandise trade decreased (by 7.4 per cent) for the second year after two consecutive years of growth. Global exports amounted to US$17.6 trillion, US$1.4 trillion less than the previous year reflecting the effects of COVID-19. Despite the challenges of the pandemic, exports value is nowcast to recover in 2021 and grow 22.4 per cent.

Global exports were distributed in almost equal shares between the 'North' and the 'South'. In 2020, developing economies contributed US$8.1 trillion and developed economies US$9.5 trillion to the world total. Asia and Oceania accounted for 44 per cent of the world total in merchandise exports, followed by Europe with 38 per cent and America with 16 per cent. Africa remained underrepresented, capturing only 2 per cent of the world total.

Figure 1.1.1 | **World merchandise exports, quarterly**
(Trillions of United States dollars)

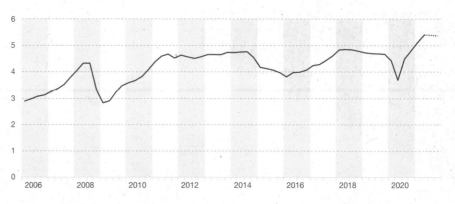

Note: Seasonally adjusted series, the dotted line indicates UNCTAD nowcasts. For the methodology, see annex 6.3. For UNCTAD's Nowcast Bulletin, see UNCTAD (2021f).

Different exposures to the downswing in trade

In 2020, merchandise exports and imports decreased considerably, between 4.4 and 19.3 per cent, in all groups of economies classified by development status.

Developing economies in Africa experienced a strong decline of exports and imports, 19.3 and 13.2 per cent, respectively, while developing economies in America saw their imports fall by 15.2 per cent and exports by 9.5 per cent.

Figure 1.1.2 | **Merchandise trade annual growth rates, 2020**
(Percentage)

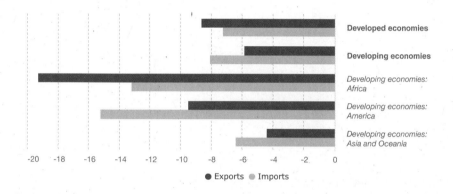

● Exports ● Imports

Development of global trade imbalances

The relatively smaller loss in developing economies' exports in 2020 was reflected in a considerable increase of their trade surplus, which had already grown continuously during the three previous years. Between 2018 and 2020, developing economies' trade balance rose from +US$421 billion to +US$582 billion.

This development was mirrored by an increase of developed economies' trade deficit between 2018 (-US$702 billion) and 2020 (-US$791 billion). In 2020, the developed world's exports declined more than its imports.

Figure 1.1.3 | **Merchandise trade balance**
(Billions of United States dollars)

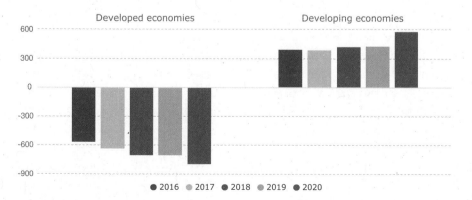

● 2016 ● 2017 ● 2018 ● 2019 ● 2020

Note: Trade balances do not add up to zero at world level due to CIF included in imports and cross-country differences in compilation methods.

In 2020, world merchandise trade **decreased by 7.4%**

Strong recovery of 22.4% nowcast for exports in 2021

Developing economies' **imports** in 2020 followed the global trend and **fell by 8%**

Trade imbalance between developing and developed world

went **up for the fourth consecutive year**

Table 1.1.1 | Merchandise trade by group of economies

Group of economies	Exports Value (Billions of US$) 2019	Exports Value (Billions of US$) 2020	Exports Annual growth rate (Percentage) 2020	Imports Value (Billions of US$) 2019	Imports Value (Billions of US$) 2020	Imports Annual growth rate (Percentage) 2020	Trade balance Value (Billions of US$) 2020	Trade balance Ratio to imports (Percentage) 2020
World	**19 019**	**17 619**	**-7.4**	**19 290**	**17 828**	**-7.6**	**-209**	**-1.2**
Developed economies	10 426	9 527	-8.6	11 123	10 319	-7.2	-791	-7.7
Developing economies	8 593	8 092	-5.8	8 166	7 509	-8.0	582	7.8
Developing economies: Africa	479	386	-19.3	586	509	-13.2	-123	-24.1
Developing economies: America	1 055	955	-9.5	1 082	917	-15.2	37	4.1
Developing economies: Asia and Oceania	7 060	6 750	-4.4	6 498	6 083	-6.4	668	11.0
Selected groups								
Developing economies excluding China	6 094	5 501	-9.7	6 088	5 452	-10.4	49	0.9
Developing economies excluding LDCs	8 394	7 911	-5.8	7 887	7 262	-7.9	649	8.9
LDCs	199	181	-9.1	279	248	-11.2	-67	-26.9
LLDCs	190	167	-11.8	227	206	-9.3	-38	-18.7
SIDS (UN-OHRLLS)	458	419	-8.4	469	417	-11.1	2	0.5
HIPCs (IMF)	133	129	-3.0	181	161	-11.0	-32	-19.9
BRICS	3 559	3 494	-1.8	3 111	2 921	-6.1	574	19.6
G20	14 598	13 566	-7.1	14 878	13 766	-7.5	-200	-1.5

Table 1.1.2 | Merchandise trade of least developed countries, main exporters

Economy[a]	Exports Value (Millions of US$) 2019	Exports Value (Millions of US$) 2020	Exports Annual growth rate (Percentage) 2020	Imports Value (Millions of US$) 2019	Imports Value (Millions of US$) 2020	Imports Annual growth rate (Percentage) 2020	Trade balance Value (Millions of US$) 2020	Trade balance Ratio to imports (Percentage) 2020
LDCs	**198 941**	**180 843**	**-9.1**	**278 631**	**247 539**	**-11.2**	**-66 696**	**-26.9**
LDCs: Africa and Haiti	116 355	103 099	-11.4	142 137	125 276	-11.9	-22 177	-17.7
Angola	34 726	20 937	-39.7	14 127	9 543	-32.4	11 394	119.4
Congo, Dem. Rep. of the	13 382	14 122	5.5	8 825	6 663	-24.5	7 459	111.9
Zambia	7 047	7 819	10.9	7 180	5 323	-25.9	2 496	46.9
Tanzania, United Republic of	5 005	6 061	21.1	9 452	7 889	-16.5	-1 828	-23.2
Guinea	3 945	(e) 5 595	(e) 41.8	3 470	(e) 3 374	(e) -2.8	(e) 2 221	(e) 65.8
LDCs: Asia	81 906	77 070	-5.9	134 737	120 578	-10.5	-43 508	-36.1
Bangladesh	39 337	33 605	-14.6	59 094	52 804	-10.6	-19 199	-36.4
Cambodia	14 825	(e) 17 215	(e) 16.1	20 279	(e) 19 131	(e) -5.7	(e) -1 916	(e) -10.0
Myanmar	17 997	16 692	-7.3	18 588	17 947	-3.4	-1 256	-7.0
Lao People's Dem. Rep.	5 806	6 115	5.3	6 272	5 370	-14.4	745	13.9
Yemen	(e) 1 435	(e) 1 204	(e) -16.1	(e) 10 407	(e) 7 399	(e) -28.9	(e) -6 195	(e) -83.7
LDCs: Islands	680	673	-0.9	1 757	1 685	-4.1	-1 012	-60.0
Solomon Islands	461	366	-20.6	(e) 590	(e) 477	(e) -19.2	(e) -111	(e) -23.3
Timor-Leste	154	264	71.4	591	625	5.9	-362	-57.9
Comoros	39	21	-47.4	265	280	5.8	-259	-92.6
Sao Tome and Principe	13	14	6.0	148	(e) 136	(e) -7.7	(e) -122	(e) -89.8
Kiribati	12	9	-24.1	132	133	0.9	-124	-93.0

[a] Ranked by value of exports in 2020.

Table 1.1.3 | **Leading exporters and importers in developing economies, by group of economies, 2020**

Developing economies: Africa

Exporter (Ranked by value)	Value (Billions of US$)	Share in world total (Percentage)	Annual growth rate (Percentage)	Importer (Ranked by value)	Value (Billions of US$)	Share in world total (Percentage)	Annual growth rate (Percentage)
South Africa	86	0.49	-4.6	South Africa	(e) 84	(e) 0.47	(e) -21.8
Nigeria	36	0.20	-43.0	Egypt	60	0.34	-15.6
Morocco	27	0.15	-6.8	Nigeria	55	0.31	0.2
Egypt	27	0.15	-8.2	Morocco	44	0.25	-13.6
Algeria	22	0.12	-39.7	Algeria	35	0.20	-16.2
Developing Africa	**386**	**2.19**	**-19.3**	**Developing Africa**	**509**	**2.85**	**-13.2**

Developing economies: America

Exporter (Ranked by value)	Value (Billions of US$)	Share in world total (Percentage)	Annual growth rate (Percentage)	Importer (Ranked by value)	Value (Billions of US$)	Share in world total (Percentage)	Annual growth rate (Percentage)
Mexico	418	2.37	-9.3	Mexico	393	2.21	-15.9
Brazil	210	1.19	-6.9	Brazil	166	0.93	-9.8
Chile	73	0.42	6.9	Chile	59	0.33	-15.3
Argentina	55	0.31	-15.7	Colombia	43	0.24	-17.5
Peru	42	0.24	-11.1	Argentina	42	0.24	-13.8
Developing America	**955**	**5.42**	**-9.5**	**Developing America**	**917**	**5.15**	**-15.2**

Developing economies: Asia and Oceania

Exporter (Ranked by value)	Value (Billions of US$)	Share in world total (Percentage)	Annual growth rate (Percentage)	Importer (Ranked by value)	Value (Billions of US$)	Share in world total (Percentage)	Annual growth rate (Percentage)
China	2 590	14.70	3.6	China	2 057	11.54	-1.0
China, Hong Kong SAR	549	3.11	2.6	China, Hong Kong SAR	570	3.20	-1.4
Korea, Republic of	512	2.91	-5.5	Korea, Republic of	468	2.62	-7.1
Singapore	363	2.06	-7.2	India	373	2.09	-23.3
China, Taiwan Province of	347	1.97	5.0	Singapore	330	1.85	-8.2
Developing Asia and Oceania	**6 750**	**38.31**	**-4.4**	**Developing Asia and Oceania**	**6 083**	**34.12**	**-6.4**

1.2 Trade structure by partner

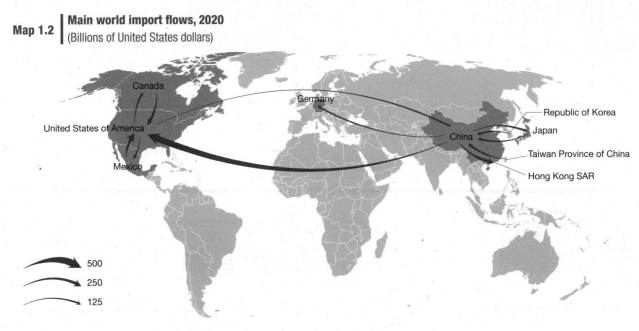

Map 1.2 | **Main world import flows, 2020**
(Billions of United States dollars)

Note: Bilateral imports of US$125 billion or more are shown.

Concepts and definitions

Intra-trade is the trade between economies belonging to the same group. Extra-trade is the trade of economies of the same group with all economies outside the group. It represents the difference between a group's total trade and intra-trade.

In theory, the exports from an economy A to an economy B, should equal the imports of economy B from economy A recorded FOB. In practice, however, the values of both flows are often different. The reasons for these trade asymmetries include: different times of recording, different treatment of transit trade, underreporting, measurement errors and mis-pricing or mis-invoicing.

The exports to (imports from) all economies of the world do not always exactly add up to total exports (imports). The difference is caused by ship stores, bunkers and other exports of minor importance.

Main global trade patterns

The world's largest bilateral flows of merchandise trade run between China and the United States of America, and between their respective neighbouring economies. In 2020, goods worth US$457 billion were imported by the United States from China. Goods worth US$136 billion also travelled in the opposite direction. China's trade – exports and imports – with Hong Kong Special Administrative Region (SAR), Japan, Taiwan, Province of China, and the Republic of Korea totalled US$1.15 trillion. The United States' trade with Mexico and Canada was worth about the same amount (US$1.07 trillion).

Intra-regional trade was most pronounced in Europe. In 2020, 68 per cent of all European exports were to trading partners on the same continent. In Asia, this rate was 58 per cent. By contrast, in Oceania, Latin America and the Caribbean, Africa and Northern America, most trade was extra-regional.

Figure 1.2.1 | **Intra- and extra-regional exports, 2020**
(Percentage of total exports)

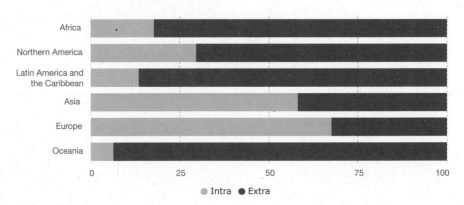

Trade within and between 'hemispheres'

In 2020, goods worth US$6.6 trillion were exchanged between developed economies (North-North trade), whereas merchandise trade among developing economies (South-South trade) amounted to US$4.6 trillion. Exports from developed to developing economies and vice-versa (North-South, and South-North trade) totaled US$6.1 trillion. Thus, for developed economies, trade with developing economies was almost as important as trade with developed economies.

Figure 1.2.2 | **Global trade flows, 2020**

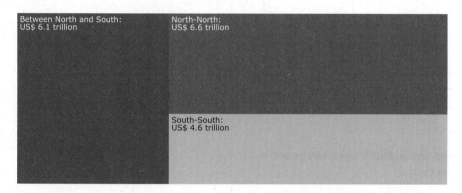

Note: North refers to developed economies, South to developing economies; trade is measured from the export side; deliveries to ship stores and bunkers as well as minor and special-category exports with unspecified destination are not included.

With whom do developing economies mainly trade?

In 2020, developing economies shipped most of their exports to the United States of America (US$1.4 trillion), followed by China (US$1.1 trillion) and other Asian economies. They also sourced most of their imports from those economies.

Exports from American developing economies were more oriented towards the Americas, especially to the United States of America (US$415 billion). For African developing economies, main export markets were in Asia and Europe, with China (US$52.9 billion) and India (US$23.0 billion) as main destinations.

Figure 1.2.3 | **Developing economies' main export destinations, 2020**
(Billions of United States dollars)

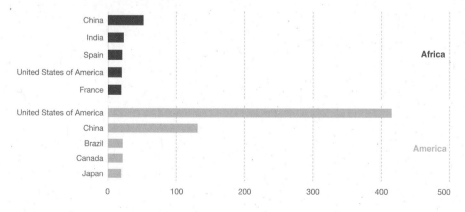

United States
of America
traded
US$1.1 trillion
with Canada and
Mexico in 2020

**58% of Asia's trade
is intra-regional**

**South-South trade
still lower**
compared to its
extra-trade:

US$4.6
trillion

The **United States
and China** are the
main markets

for developing
economies' exports

Table 1.2.1 | **Exports by origin and destination, 2020**
(Billions of United States dollars)

Origin	Destination					
	World	Developed economies	Developing economies			
			Total	Africa	America	Asia and Oceania
World	**17 473**	**10 015**	**7 332**	**538**	**882**	**5 912**
	(100)	(57)	(42)	(3)	(5)	(34)
Developed economies	9 382	6 585	2 703	209	508	1 986
	(100)	(70)	(29)	(2)	(5)	(21)
Developing economies	8 092	3 430	4 629	329	374	3 925
	(100)	(42)	(57)	(4)	(5)	(49)
Developing economies: Africa	388	165	214	69	7	138
	(100)	(42)	(55)	(18)	(2)	(36)
Developing economies: America	953	565	370	14	131	225
	(100)	(59)	(39)	(2)	(14)	(24)
Developing economies: Asia and Oceania	6 751	2 700	4 045	246	237	3 562
	(100)	(40)	(60)	(4)	(4)	(53)

Note: Percentage of exports to the whole world in parentheses.

Table 1.2.2 | **Exports by origin and destination, selected years**
(Billions of United States dollars)

Origin	Year	Destination					
		World	Developed economies	Developing economies			
				Total	Africa	America	Asia and Oceania
World	2010	15 116	8 961	6 025	483	870	4 672
	2015	16 386	9 176	7 049	566	974	5 509
	2020	17 473	10 015	7 332	538	882	5 912
Developed economies	2010	8 604	6 042	2 454	227	494	1 733
	2015	8 886	6 080	2 680	225	578	1 876
	2020	9 382	6 585	2 703	209	508	1 986
Developing economies	2010	6 512	2 919	3 571	256	376	2 939
	2015	7 499	3 096	4 369	341	396	3 632
	2020	8 092	3 430	4 629	329	374	3 925
Developing economies: Africa	2010	513	295	214	70	16	128
	2015	394	185	202	72	11	119
	2020	388	165	214	69	7	138
Developing economies: America	2010	891	538	346	16	178	152
	2015	917	567	341	15	158	168
	2020	953	565	370	14	131	225
Developing economies: Asia and Oceania	2010	5 107	2 086	3 010	170	181	2 659
	2015	6 188	2 343	3 826	254	226	3 345
	2020	6 751	2 700	4 045	246	237	3 562

Table 1.2.3 | **Top destinations of developing economies' exports**

Destination (Ranked by value of exports)	Rank		2020		
	2020	2015	Value	Share in total exports	Cumulative share
			(Billions of US$)	(Percentage)	(Percentage)
United States of America	1	1	1 364	16.9	16.9
China	2	2	1 097	13.6	30.4
China, Hong Kong SAR	3	3	484	6.0	36.4
Japan	4	4	394	4.9	41.3
Korea, Republic of	5	5	264	3.3	44.5
India	6	6	259	3.2	47.7
Viet Nam	7	10	238	2.9	50.7
Germany	8	8	206	2.5	53.2
Singapore	9	7	202	2.5	55.7
Netherlands	10	11	187	2.3	58.0
United Kingdom	11	12	169	2.1	60.1
China, Taiwan Province of	12	9	164	2.0	62.1
Malaysia	13	14	155	1.9	64.0
Thailand	14	16	138	1.7	65.7
United Arab Emirates	15	13	127	1.6	67.3
Rest of the world	-	-	**2 644**	**32.7**	**100.0**
World	-	-	**8 092**	**100.0**	

Table 1.2.4 | **Top origins of developing economies' imports**

Origin (Ranked by value of imports)	Rank		2020		
	2020	2015	Value	Share in total imports	Cumulative share
			(Billions of US$)	(Percentage)	(Percentage)
China	1	1	1 240	16.6	16.6
United States of America	2	2	748	10.0	26.7
Japan	3	3	477	6.4	33.1
Korea, Republic of	4	4	392	5.3	38.3
China, Taiwan Province of	5	6	378	5.1	43.4
Germany	6	5	290	3.9	47.3
Malaysia	7	8	221	3.0	50.3
Australia	8	10	190	2.5	52.8
Viet Nam	9	21	176	2.4	55.2
Singapore	10	7	176	2.4	57.5
India	11	9	164	2.2	59.7
Brazil	12	14	163	2.2	61.9
Russian Federation	13	16	153	2.1	64.0
Thailand	14	11	152	2.0	66.0
United Arab Emirates	15	17	139	1.9	67.9
Rest of the world	-	-	**2 392**	**32.1**	**100.0**
World	-	-	**7 451**	**100.0**	

1.3 Trade structure by product

Map 1.3 | **Main export products, 2020**

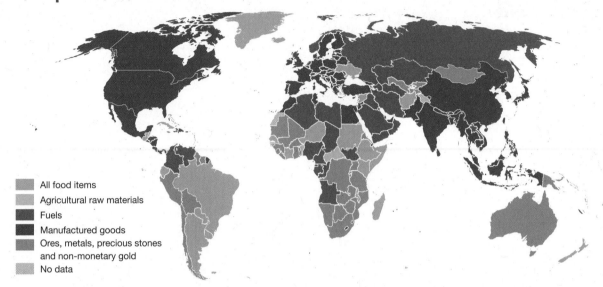

- All food items
- Agricultural raw materials
- Fuels
- Manufactured goods
- Ores, metals, precious stones and non-monetary gold
- No data

Concepts and definitions

The breakdown of merchandise trade by product group is based on the entries in the customs declarations that are coded in accordance with a globally harmonized classification system, called the Harmonized Commodity Description and Coding System (HS). The values of the individual customs declarations have been summed up to the level of product group, error-checked and submitted to the United Nations Statistics Division for integration in the UN Comtrade database (United Nations, 2021).

The UN Comtrade database contains product breakdowns based on the Standard International Trade Classification (SITC). These have been obtained by conversion of the raw data coded in HS and constitute the main source of the figures presented in this section. For correspondence between SITC codes and the five broad product groups presented in this section, see annex 6.2.

Regional specialization patterns

The supply of goods to the world market has a regional pattern. According to 2020 figures, economies in Northern and Central America, Europe and Southern, Eastern and South-Eastern Asia export mainly manufactured goods. The main fuel exporters are located along the northern coast of South America, in Middle and Northern Africa and Western and Central Asia. Some other countries, for example Madagascar, Niger, Somalia, Ukraine and Brazil, specialized in food in 2020.

In Africa, primary goods accounted for 75 per cent of merchandise exports in 2020; of which fuels made up 39 per cent. Developing Asia and Oceania relied much less on primary goods in their exports (21 per cent). Developing America recorded the largest proportion of food exports (25 per cent) among the three developing regions.

Figure 1.3.1 | **Export structure of developing economies by product group, 2020**
(Percentage)

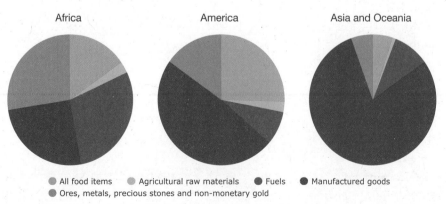

Africa | America | Asia and Oceania

- All food items
- Agricultural raw materials
- Fuels
- Manufactured goods
- Ores, metals, precious stones and non-monetary gold

Note: Non-allocated products are not considered.

Decline in trade for several products

The contraction of world merchandise trade in 2020 (see section 1.1) during the COVID-19 pandemic was strongly driven by fuel price collapse. The export of fuels fell sharply, by 33 per cent. Exports of agricultural raw materials decreased by 6 per cent and those of manufactured goods by 4 per cent. Exports of ores, metals, precious stones and non-monetary gold grew by 6 per cent and trade in food increased by almost 2 per cent.

Figure 1.3.2 | **Annual growth rate of exports by product group, 2020**
(Percentage)

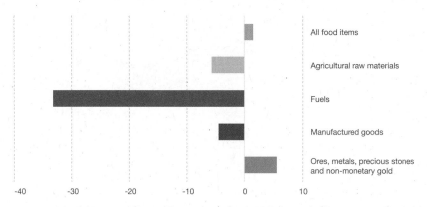

What do developing regions trade with others?

Developing regions show considerable differences in their respective trade with the rest of the world. In 2020, economies in Asia and Oceania recorded a merchandise trade surplus of 10 per cent driven by high exports of manufactured goods. In America, high imports of manufactured goods were partially offset by food exports. Overall, the region had a 7 per cent trade surplus. In contrast, the trade structure was entirely different in Africa, with imports of manufactured goods three times higher than exports. Although counterbalanced by surpluses in ores, metals, precious stones, monetary gold and in fuels, an overall deficit as large as 25 per cent remained. Developing America showed comparably high net-exports of food.

Figure 1.3.3 | **Developing economies' extra-trade structure, 2020**
(Percentage of exports)

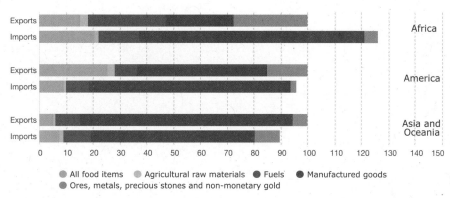

Note: Non-allocated products are not considered.

Manufacturing exporters are mostly in

Northern America   Europe   South and East Asia

$\frac{3}{4}$ **of Africa's** merchandise **exports** are **primary goods**

World **fuels** trade **dropped** by 33% in 2020

Africa imported 3 times more manufactured goods than it exported in 2020

Table 1.3 | **Exports by product group, origin and destination, 2020**
(Millions of United States dollars)

All food items

Origin	Destination					
	World	Developed economies	Developing economies			
			Total	Africa	America	Asia and Oceania
World	**1 581 569**	**916 364**	**663 485**	**86 349**	**81 758**	**495 379**
	(100)	(58)	(42)	(5)	(5)	(31)
Developed economies	946 990	666 401	279 643	36 877	44 863	197 903
	(100)	(70)	(30)	(4)	(5)	(21)
Developing economies	634 579	249 963	383 842	49 472	36 895	297 476
	(100)	(39)	(60)	(8)	(6)	(47)
Developing economies: Africa	59 249	28 030	31 174	14 871	447	15 857
	(100)	(47)	(53)	(25)	(1)	(27)
Developing economies: America	231 068	107 423	123 022	10 886	30 949	81 186
	(100)	(46)	(53)	(5)	(13)	(35)
Developing economies: Asia and Oceania	344 262	114 510	229 646	23 715	5 499	200 432
	(100)	(33)	(67)	(7)	(2)	(58)

Note: Percentage of exports to the whole world in parentheses.

Agricultural raw materials

Origin	Destination					
	World	Developed economies	Developing economies			
			Total	Africa	America	Asia and Oceania
World	**235 230**	**117 130**	**117 443**	**6 344**	**8 254**	**102 845**
	(100)	(50)	(50)	(3)	(4)	(44)
Developed economies	145 477	89 088	56 345	3 807	5 448	47 090
	(100)	(61)	(39)	(3)	(4)	(32)
Developing economies	89 753	28 041	61 098	2 537	2 806	55 755
	(100)	(31)	(68)	(3)	(3)	(62)
Developing economies: Africa	10 780	3 376	7 399	923	69	6 407
	(100)	(31)	(69)	(9)	(1)	(59)
Developing economies: America	24 082	9 480	13 994	134	1 509	12 352
	(100)	(39)	(58)	(1)	(6)	(51)
Developing economies: Asia and Oceania	54 891	15 185	39 704	1 480	1 228	36 996
	(100)	(28)	(72)	(3)	(2)	(67)

Note: Percentage of exports to the whole world in parentheses.

Fuels

Origin	Destination					
	World	Developed economies	Developing economies			
			Total	Africa	America	Asia and Oceania
World	**1 496 044**	**667 991**	**792 961**	**61 150**	**89 168**	**642 643**
	(100)	(45)	(53)	(4)	(6)	(43)
Developed economies	685 892	431 079	233 507	23 107	62 994	147 406
	(100)	(63)	(34)	(3)	(9)	(21)
Developing economies	810 152	236 912	559 454	38 043	26 174	495 237
	(100)	(29)	(69)	(5)	(3)	(61)
Developing economies: Africa	112 196	47 285	63 708	11 882	2 734	49 093
	(100)	(42)	(57)	(11)	(2)	(44)
Developing economies: America	75 711	17 860	47 009	478	17 386	29 144
	(100)	(24)	(62)	(1)	(23)	(38)
Developing economies: Asia and Oceania	622 245	171 766	448 736	25 683	6 054	417 000
	(100)	(28)	(72)	(4)	(1)	(67)

Note: Percentage of exports to the whole world in parentheses.

Manufactured goods

Origin	Destination					
	World	Developed economies	Developing economies			
			Total	Africa	America	Asia and Oceania
World	**12 373 833**	**7 387 749**	**4 975 221**	**350 070**	**642 891**	**3 982 260**
	(100)	(60)	(40)	(3)	(5)	(32)
Developed economies	6 534 214	4 757 409	1 767 707	132 618	358 299	1 276 790
	(100)	(73)	(27)	(2)	(6)	(20)
Developing economies	5 839 620	2 630 340	3 207 514	217 452	284 592	2 705 471
	(100)	(45)	(55)	(4)	(5)	(46)
Developing economies: Africa	97 870	48 836	48 919	30 642	3 228	15 050
	(100)	(50)	(50)	(31)	(3)	(15)
Developing economies: America	441 060	352 955	87 444	1 711	67 261	18 472
	(100)	(80)	(20)	(0)	(15)	(4)
Developing economies: Asia and Oceania	5 300 690	2 228 549	3 071 151	185 099	214 103	2 671 949
	(100)	(42)	(58)	(4)	(4)	(50)

Note: Percentage of exports to the whole world in parentheses.

Ores, metals, precious stones and non-monetary gold

Origin	Destination					
	World	Developed economies	Developing economies			
			Total	Africa	America	Asia and Oceania
World	**1 264 920**	**641 934**	**614 172**	**23 352**	**20 309**	**570 511**
	(100)	(51)	(49)	(2)	(2)	(45)
Developed economies	651 169	408 137	241 523	5 928	10 976	224 619
	(100)	(63)	(37)	(1)	(2)	(34)
Developing economies	613 751	233 796	372 649	17 424	9 334	345 892
	(100)	(38)	(61)	(3)	(2)	(56)
Developing economies: Africa	106 392	36 713	62 959	10 754	382	51 823
	(100)	(35)	(59)	(10)	(0)	(49)
Developing economies: America	136 835	52 692	83 584	619	5 375	77 590
	(100)	(39)	(61)	(0)	(4)	(57)
Developing economies: Asia and Oceania	370 523	144 391	226 106	6 051	3 577	216 479
	(100)	(39)	(61)	(2)	(1)	(58)

Note: Percentage of exports to the whole world in parentheses.

1.4 Trade indicators

Map 1.4 | **Trade openness index, 2020**
(Percentage)

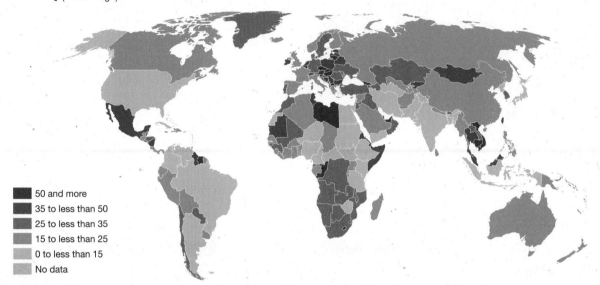

- 50 and more
- 35 to less than 50
- 25 to less than 35
- 15 to less than 25
- 0 to less than 15
- No data

Note: This index measures the relative importance of international trade in goods relative to the domestic economic output of an economy. Exports are given equal weight to imports.

Concepts and definitions

This section presents different indices that can be used to analyze trade flows and trade patterns over time from the perspective of, for example, relative competitiveness, structure of global exports and imports markets, or the importance of trade for the economy, both for individual economies and for groups of economies.

For information on how the indices in this section are calculated, see annex 6.3. The presented indices are a subset of the trade indices available at UNCTADstat (UNCTAD, 2021a).

How important is trade for economies?

In 2020, the economies most open to international trade, as measured by the ratio of the mean of exports and imports of goods to gross domestic product (GDP), were relatively small economies in South-Eastern Asia and Eastern Europe, including China, Hong Kong SAR (151 per cent), Singapore (104 per cent), and Slovakia (76 per cent). By contrast, China, the United States of America and Japan recorded ratios of 15 per cent or below. The lowest value, 3 per cent, was reported for Zimbabwe. Cuba and Iran ranked as the second and third least open economies, respectively.

How did the relative price of exports to imports develop?

In 2020, almost all geographical regions, except Asia and Oceania, saw their terms of trade fall. The largest decline of 6.6 per cent was recorded in the African region, followed by North America (-1.4 per cent) and Latin America and Caribbean (-1.2 per cent). The terms of trade of European countries stood at 99.4 points.

Figure 1.4.1 | **Terms of trade index**
(2015=100)

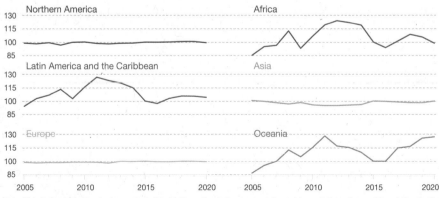

Note: This index indicates by how much the relative price between exports and imports has changed in relation to the base year.

How concentrated is global product supply?

Large differences persisted in the degree to which global supply was concentrated among exporting economies. In 2020, the most unequally distributed group, by far, was manufactured products, as indicated by a market concentration index of 0.20, as compared to index values between 0.12 and 0.15 recorded for the other product groups. The concentration index of food has followed a declining trend since 2013, but changed direction in 2020, with a 1.9 per cent increase as compared to 2019. For fuels, a considerable increase in the concentration of world market supply was observed over the last two years.

Figure 1.4.2 | **Market concentration index of exports**

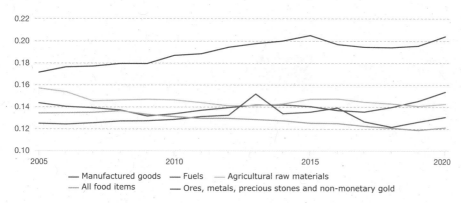

— Manufactured goods — Fuels — Agricultural raw materials
— All food items — Ores, metals, precious stones and non-monetary gold

Note: This index measures the extent to which a high proportion of exports are delivered by a small number of economies. It has a value of 1 if all exports originate from a single economy.

How did the volume of trade change?

The volume of world merchandise exports and imports shrank by approximately 5.5 per cent in 2020, corresponding to the developments of the value of merchandise trade (see section 1.1). The decline in export volume was significantly stronger in developed (-8.0 per cent) than developing economies (-2.5 per cent), leading in developed economies to a volume 1.4 per cent lower than in 2015. During the same period, imports in volume terms were down by 6.5 per cent in developed regions and 4.2 per cent in developing regions.

Figure 1.4.3 | **Volume index of exports and imports**
(2015=100)

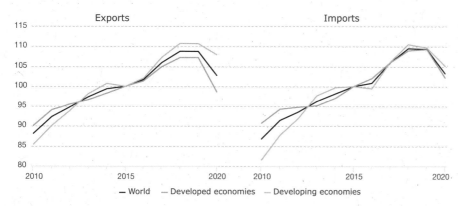

— World — Developed economies — Developing economies

Note: This index indicates the change in exports or imports, adjusted for the movement of prices, relative to the base year.

Hong Kong SAR ranks **highest** in trade-openness;

Zimbabwe is placed at the **bottom**

Africa's terms of trade fell by 6.6% in 2020

-6.6%

In 2020, **market concentration** of exports **increased** in all product groups

---

Volumes of global **merchandise** trade plunged by **5.5%** in 2020

Table 1.4.1 | **Selected trade indices by group of economies**
(2015=100)

Developed economies

Year	Volume[a]		Purchasing power of exports[b]	Terms of trade[c]
	Imports	Exports		
2010	91	90	90	100
2018	109	107	108	101
2019	109	107	108	101
2020	102	99	100	101

[a] See note, figure 1.4.3 above.
[b] This index indicates the change in exports, valuated in prices of imports, relative to the base year.
[c] See note, figure 1.4.1 above.

Developing economies

Year	Volume[a]		Purchasing power of exports[b]	Terms of trade[c]
	Imports	Exports		
2010	82	85	83	98
2018	111	111	111	100
2019	110	111	110	99
2020	105	108	108	100

Developing economies: Africa

Year	Volume[a]		Purchasing power of exports[b]	Terms of trade[c]
	Imports	Exports		
2010	76	111	118	107
2018	95	111	120	109
2019	97	110	116	106
2020	86	97	96	99

[a] See note, figure 1.4.3 above.
[b] This index indicates the change in exports, valuated in prices of imports, relative to the base year.
[c] See note, figure 1.4.1 above.

Developing economies: America

Year	Volume[a]		Purchasing power of exports[b]	Terms of trade[c]
	Imports	Exports		
2010	88	85	98	116
2018	105	107	113	106
2019	103	106	112	105
2020	90	101	105	104

Developing economies: Asia and Oceania

Year	Volume[a]		Purchasing power of exports[b]	Terms of trade[c]
	Imports	Exports		
2010	81	83	79	95
2018	113	112	110	98
2019	112	112	109	98
2020	110	110	109	99

[a] See note, figure 1.4.3 above.
[b] This index indicates the change in exports, valuated in prices of imports, relative to the base year.
[c] See note, figure 1.4.1 above.

Table 1.4.2 | **Selected trade indices, landlocked developing countries**
(2015=100)

Economy	Volume[a]				Purchasing power of exports[b]		Terms of trade[c]	
	Imports		Exports					
	2019	2020	2019	2020	2019	2020	2019	2020
Afghanistan	85	92	130	107	147	127	113	119
Armenia	170	145	156	147	177	177	114	120
Azerbaijan	142	109	101	96	113	76	112	80
Bhutan	86	80	103	106	115	112	111	106
Bolivia (Plurinational State of)	85	62	86	70	85	69	99	98
Botswana	89	91	86	73	81	69	95	94
Burkina Faso	131	129	124	142	140	194	112	137
Burundi	100	103	136	108	144	130	106	120
Central African Republic	167	163	176	144	165	137	93	95
Chad	68	68	108	128	125	101	116	79
Eswatini	123	102	117	95	105	88	89	93
Ethiopia	85	75	99	112	92	107	93	96
Kazakhstan	118	114	105	105	119	94	113	90
Kyrgyzstan	117	88	118	104	131	136	112	130
Lao People's Dem. Rep.	104	90	134	145	150	159	112	110
Lesotho	92	83	113	95	104	87	92	92
Malawi	124	116	87	75	82	68	94	91
Mali	127	124	114	100	127	139	112	140
Moldova, Republic of	141	139	138	115	136	129	98	113
Mongolia	152	134	124	136	153	156	124	115
Nepal	174	139	138	106	126	111	91	104
Niger	112	110	109	87	98	84	90	96
North Macedonia	140	126	155	141	150	136	97	96
Paraguay	106	89	85	93	79	92	94	99
Rwanda	106	99	161	165	172	191	107	116
Tajikistan	92	88	111	137	125	152	112	111
Turkmenistan	40	42	130	117	94	60	72	51
Uganda	131	136	147	154	148	167	100	108
Uzbekistan	182	166	133	122	142	133	107	108
Zambia	84	62	99	108	99	110	100	102
Zimbabwe	76	78	121	118	125	128	103	109

[a] See note, figure 1.4.3 above.
[b] See footnote "b", table 1.4.1 above.
[c] See note, figure 1.4.1 above.

2

International trade in services

KEY FIGURES 2020

Value of world
services exports
US$5 trillion

Change of world
services exports
-20.0%

Share of travel in
world services
exports
11%

NOWCAST 2021

Growth of global
services exports
+13.6%

2.1 Total trade in services

Map 2.1 | **Exports of services as a ratio to gross domestic product, 2020**
(Percentage)

- 20 and more
- 10 to less than 20
- 3 to less than 10
- 0 to less than 3
- No data

Concepts and definitions

In this chapter, in accordance with the concepts of the balance of payments (International Monetary Fund, 2009) and national accounts (United Nations et al., 2009), services are understood as the result of a production activity that changes the conditions of the consuming units, or facilitates the exchange of products or financial assets.

International trade in services takes place when a service is supplied in any of the following modes: from one economy to another (services cross the border); within an economy to service a consumer of another economy (consumer crosses the border); or through the presence of natural persons of one economy in another economy (supplier crosses the border) (United Nations et al., 2012).

Trade-in-services figures are jointly compiled by UNCTAD and WTO, in cooperation with ITC and UNSD.

Seasonal adjustments are based on UNCTAD secretariat calculations using X-11.

Heavily hit in 2020, recovering in 2021

After the pandemic-driven decline of 20 per cent in 2020, world services exports have been on a recovery path over the first six months of 2021. Growth of 23 per cent year-on-year is nowcast for the third quarter of 2021, and 13.6 per cent growth is nowcast for the whole of 2021 compared with 2020.

In 2020, global services exports were valued at US$5 trillion, representing 5.9 per cent of world GDP and 22.6 per cent of total world trade in both goods and services. Given the weaker resilience of services trade – travel in particular - to the pandemic conditions, exports of services lost more ground than goods' exports in 2020. Yet, in more than a third of the world's economies, services exports' share in GDP surpassed 10 per cent. Luxembourg and Malta recorded services exports higher than 100 per cent of their GDP. Many small island states, for which international tourism is important, saw their services exports, and their contribution to GDP, drop considerably in 2020.

Figure 2.1.1 | **World services exports, quarterly**
(Trillions of United States dollars)

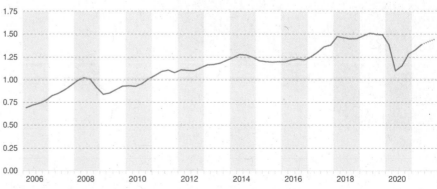

Note: Seasonally adjusted series, the dotted line indicates UNCTAD nowcasts. For the methodology, see annex 6.3. For UNCTAD's Nowcast Bulletin, see UNCTAD (2021f).

No region was spared

Looking at the trends by development status and region, a heavy decline in services exports was observed in all groups of economies. The highest relative drop was measured in American developing economies and in Africa, where travel and transport hold a more prominent role. Services imports also decreased everywhere, with the highest relative decline measured for the group of American developing economies (Latin America and the Caribbean).

Figure 2.1.2 | **Services trade annual growth rates, 2020**
(Percentage)

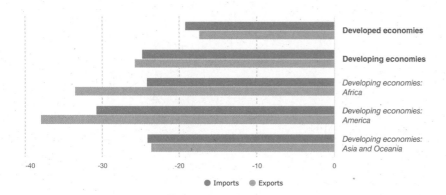

Imports ● Exports ●

Leading services exporters

With US$706 billion worth of services sold internationally in 2020, the United States of America remained the world's leading exporter, maintaining a 14 per cent share of the global market. It was followed, at some distance, by two European countries that jointly captured a 13 per cent market share. China, the leading exporter among developing economies, ranked fourth overall, with US$281 billion of services sold. All top five services exporters from the developing world were Asian. In 2020, they captured 16 per cent of the global market.

Figure 2.1.3 | **Top 5 services exporters, 2020**
(Billions of United States dollars)

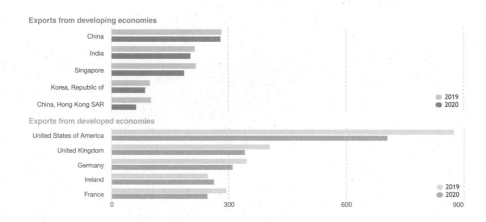

Exports from developing economies

China
India
Singapore
Korea, Republic of
China, Hong Kong SAR

● 2019
● 2020

Exports from developed economies

United States of America
United Kingdom
Germany
Ireland
France

● 2019
● 2020

0   300   600   900

Services exports nowcast to **recover by 14%** in 2021 after a 20% decline in 2020

International trade in **services accounted** for **6%** of world GDP in 2020 = 1 percentage point less than in pre-pandemic years

In 2020, developing economies' services **exports declined by 26%**

Top 5 exporters from the **developing** world

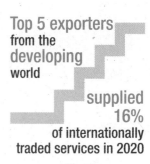

supplied 16% of internationally traded services in 2020

Table 2.1.1 | Trade in services by group of economies

Group of economies	Exports			Imports		
	Value	Share in world	Annual growth rate	Value	Share in world	Annual growth rate
	(Billions of US$)	(Percentage)	(Percentage)	(Billions of US$)	(Percentage)	(Percentage)
	2019	2020	2020	2020	2019	2020	2020	2020
World	**6 227**	**4 984**	**100.0**	**-20.0**	**5 947**	**4 681**	**100.0**	**-21.3**
Developed economies	4 333	3 578	71.8	-17.4	3 764	3 039	64.9	-19.3
Developing economies	1 894	1 406	28.2	-25.8	2 183	1 642	35.1	-24.8
Developing economies: Africa	124	83	1.7	-33.5	188	143	3.1	-24.2
Developing economies: America	200	124	2.5	-38.0	224	155	3.3	-30.7
Developing economies: Asia and Oceania	1 570	1 200	24.1	-23.6	1 771	1 344	28.7	-24.1
Selected groups							
Developing economies excluding China	1 611	1 126	22.6	-30.1	1 683	1 261	26.9	-25.0
Developing economies excluding LDCs	1 845	1 373	27.6	-25.6	2 112	1 582	33.8	-25.1
LDCs	49	33	0.7	-32.7	71	61	1.3	-14.7
LLDCs	46	30	0.6	-35.5	70	54	1.1	-23.5
SIDS (UN-OHRLLS)	290	231	4.6	-20.6	250	206	4.4	-17.7
HIPCs (IMF)	43	31	0.6	-27.5	66	59	1.3	-10.7
BRICS	610	567	11.4	-7.0	865	659	14.1	-23.8
G20	4 843	4 014	80.5	-17.1	4 596	3 659	78.2	-20.4

Table 2.1.2 | Leading services exporters and importers by group of economies, 2020

Developed economies

Exporter (Ranked by value)	Value (Billions of US$)	Share in world total (Percentage)	Annual growth rate (Percentage)
United States of America	706	14.2	-19.5
United Kingdom	342	6.9	-15.5
Germany	311	6.2	-10.4
Ireland	263	5.3	6.0
France	246	4.9	-16.5
Developed economies	**3 578**	**71.8**	**-17.4**

Importer (Ranked by value)	Value (Billions of US$)	Share in world total (Percentage)	Annual growth rate (Percentage)
United States of America	460	9.8	-22.1
Germany	309	6.6	-16.8
Ireland	296	6.3	-11.0
France	232	4.9	-14.2
United Kingdom	205	4.4	-26.2
Developed economies	**3 039**	**64.9**	**-19.3**

Developing economies

Exporter (Ranked by value)	Value (Billions of US$)	Share in world total (Percentage)	Annual growth rate (Percentage)
China	281	5.6	-0.9
India	203	4.1	-5.4
Singapore	188	3.8	-13.6
Korea, Republic of	(e) 87	(e) 1.8	(e) -12.0
China, Hong Kong SAR	64	1.3	-37.4
Developing economies	**1 406**	**28.2**	**-25.8**

Importer (Ranked by value)	Value (Billions of US$)	Share in world total (Percentage)	Annual growth rate (Percentage)
China	381	8.1	-23.9
Singapore	173	3.7	-17.1
India	(e) 154	(e) 3.3	(e) -14.2
Korea, Republic of	(e) 103	(e) 2.2	(e) -18.8
United Arab Emirates	60	1.3	-32.5
Developing economies	**1 642**	**35.1**	**-24.8**

Developing economies: Africa

Exporter (Ranked by value)	Value (Billions of US$)	Share in world total (Percentage)	Annual growth rate (Percentage)
Egypt	15	0.3	-39.9
Morocco	14	0.3	-28.4
Ghana	(e) 8	(e) 0.2	(e) -18.4
South Africa	8	0.2	-48.9
Ethiopia	4	0.1	-7.9
Developing Africa	**83**	**1.7**	**-33.5**

Importer (Ranked by value)	Value (Billions of US$)	Share in world total (Percentage)	Annual growth rate (Percentage)
Nigeria	20	0.4	-48.8
Egypt	18	0.4	-14.1
Ghana	(e) 13	(e) 0.3	(e) -7.2
South Africa	10	0.2	-37.1
Algeria	(e) 8	(e) 0.2	(e) -19.5
Developing Africa	**143**	**3.1**	**-24.2**

Developing economies: America

Exporter (Ranked by value)	Value (Billions of US$)	Share in world total (Percentage)	Annual growth rate (Percentage)
Brazil	28	0.6	-16.9
Mexico	(e) 17	(e) 0.3	(e) -46.1
Argentina	9	0.2	-33.5
Panama	9	0.2	-38.6
Costa Rica	(e) 7	(e) 0.1	(e) -28.8
Developing America	**124**	**2.5**	**-38.0**

Importer (Ranked by value)	Value (Billions of US$)	Share in world total (Percentage)	Annual growth rate (Percentage)
Brazil	49	1.0	-29.6
Mexico	(e) 25	(e) 0.5	(e) -32.2
Argentina	12	0.3	-39.2
Chile	11	0.2	-21.2
Colombia	(e) 9	(e) 0.2	(e) -33.7
Developing America	**155**	**3.3**	**-30.7**

Developing economies: Asia and Oceania

Exporter (Ranked by value)	Value (Billions of US$)	Share in world total (Percentage)	Annual growth rate (Percentage)
China	281	5.6	-0.9
India	203	4.1	-5.4
Singapore	188	3.8	-13.6
Korea, Republic of	(e) 87	(e) 1.8	(e) -12.0
China, Hong Kong SAR	64	1.3	-37.4
Developing Asia and Oceania	**1 200**	**24.1**	**-23.6**

Importer (Ranked by value)	Value (Billions of US$)	Share in world total (Percentage)	Annual growth rate (Percentage)
China	381	8.1	-23.9
Singapore	173	3.7	-17.1
India	(e) 154	(e) 3.3	(e) -14.2
Korea, Republic of	(e) 103	(e) 2.2	(e) -18.8
United Arab Emirates	60	1.3	-32.5
Developing Asia and Oceania	**1 344**	**28.7**	**-24.1**

2.2 Trade in services by category

Map 2.2 | **Growth in services exports by category, 2015–2020**
(Average annual growth rate*, percentage)

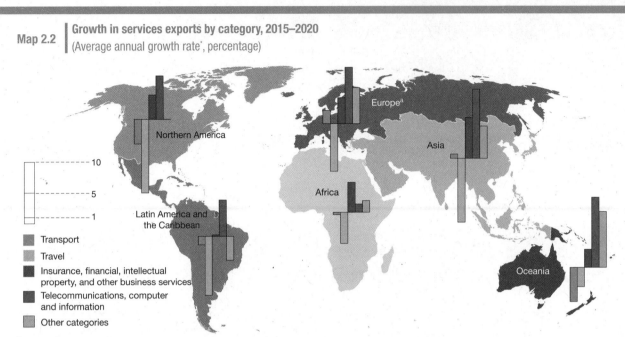

* Least squares growth rate (see annex 6.3).
a Including the Russian Federation and the French overseas departments.

Concepts and definitions

The breakdown by service category in this section has been built from the division of services in the balance of payments statistics, known as the 2010 Extended Balance of Payments Services Classification (EBOPS 2010) (United Nations et al., 2012). For the correspondence to the EBOPS 2010 categories and to the main groups presented in UNCTADstat, see annex 6.2.

The presented trade-in-services figures are jointly compiled by UNCTAD and WTO, in cooperation with ITC and UNSD.

Regional trends over five years

International trade in services, more so than goods, was heavily influenced by the COVID-19 pandemic. In 2020, the exports of travel and transport retracted across the globe. From 2015 to 2019, global services trade enjoyed growth across main services categories on all continents. Africa's travel exports rose substantially, while other regions registered solid gains in telecommunications and computer services.

As a result of the pandemic, the trends changed drastically. From 2015 to 2020, average annual growth in travel was negative everywhere, with Africa and Oceania recording the smallest relative losses. In transport exports, only Asia and Europe maintained positive growth. Financial, insurance, business, and intellectual property services remained afloat, significantly rising in Asia (6.5 per cent). Telecommunications, computer and information services' exports gained ground everywhere (by close to 10 per cent), except in Africa.

Figure 2.2.1 | **Annual growth rate of services exports, 2020**
(Percentage)

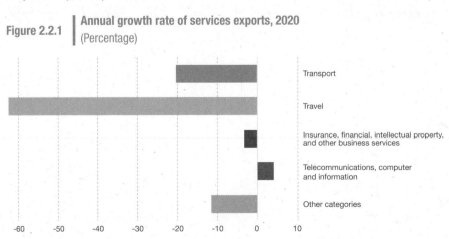

Global trends by service category

Among main service categories (figure 2.2.1), telecommunications, computer and information services were the only group recording growth in 2020 (4.1 per cent). Amid the COVID-19 pandemic, the international trade in other main categories declined. Travel was most severely affected, losing an immense 63 per cent in one year and strongly upsetting tourism-oriented economies. International transport sales - passengers and freight included - dropped by 20 per cent. Exports of business, intellectual property, financial and insurance services showed more resilience and declined by 3 per cent.

Figure 2.2.2 | Structure of services exports, 2020
(Percentage)

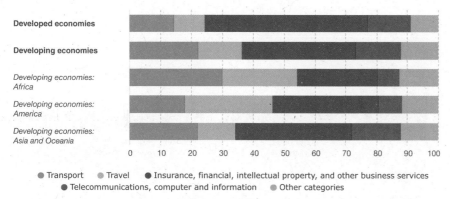

- ● Transport   ● Travel   ● Insurance, financial, intellectual property, and other business services
- ● Telecommunications, computer and information   ● Other categories

Predominance of developed economies

In 2020, over two thirds of internationally traded services were supplied by developed economies. Insurance, financial, intellectual property and other business services dominated global exports, playing a less prominent role only in Africa. Total services exports of developed economies decreased by 17 per cent in 2020. The drop was 26 per cent in developing economies, where the exports of transport and travel have a more important role.

It remains difficult for the developing world to compete in technology-intensive services markets, except for certain Asian economies. In the fastest growing main service category – telecommunications, computer and information – developing economies outside of Asia and Oceania captured just 2.2 per cent of the global market in 2020.

Figure 2.2.3 | Exports of telecommunications, computer and information services, by group of economies, 2020
(Percentage)

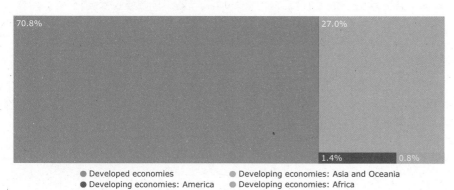

- ● Developed economies   ● Developing economies: Asia and Oceania
- ● Developing economies: America   ● Developing economies: Africa

International
travel down
by 63% in 2020

Insurance, financial,
IP and other business
services
more resilient to the
pandemic - even still
down by 3%

Since 2015,
telecommunications,
computer, and
information
services' exports
grew by 10%
annually and continued
growing during the
pandemic

African and American
developing economies
accounted for
only 2.2%
of global exports of
telecommunications,
computer and
information services

Table 2.2.1 | **Trade in services by service category and group of economies**

Developed economies

Service category	Exports			Imports			Balance	
	Value		Annual growth rate	Value		Annual growth rate		
	(Billions of US$)		(Percentage)	(Billions of US$)		(Percentage)	(Billions of US$)	
	2015	2020	2020	2015	2020	2020	2015	2020
Total services	**3 503**	**3 578**	**-17.4**	**3 005**	**3 039**	**-19.3**	**497**	**539**
Transport	568	518	-21.8	552	505	-21.8	15	13
Travel	722	348	-59.6	607	271	-63.6	115	78
Others	2 213	2 711	-3.4	1 846	2 263	-4.7	367	448

Developing economies

Service category	Exports			Imports			Balance	
	Value		Annual growth rate	Value		Annual growth rate		
	(Billions of US$)		(Percentage)	(Billions of US$)		(Percentage)	(Billions of US$)	
	2015	2020	2020	2015	2020	2020	2015	2020
Total services	**1 497**	**1 406**	**-25.8**	**1 890**	**1 642**	**-24.8**	**-393**	**-236**
Transport	328	311	-17.8	516	491	-17.4	-188	-179
Travel	482	200	-66.9	578	284	-56.9	-96	-84
Others	687	895	-1.8	796	868	-6.8	-109	27

Developing economies: Africa

Service category	Exports			Imports			Balance	
	Value		Annual growth rate	Value		Annual growth rate		
	(Billions of US$)		(Percentage)	(Billions of US$)		(Percentage)	(Billions of US$)	
	2015	2020	2020	2015	2020	2020	2015	2020
Total services	**101**	**83**	**-33.5**	**162**	**143**	**-24.2**	**-62**	**-60**
Transport	29	25	-21.4	62	55	-15.0	-33	-31
Travel	37	20	-61.0	25	16	-54.2	13	4
Others	34	38	-8.6	76	71	-18.9	-42	-33

Developing economies: America

Service category	Exports			Imports			Balance	
	Value		Annual growth rate	Value		Annual growth rate		
	(Billions of US$)		(Percentage)	(Billions of US$)		(Percentage)	(Billions of US$)	
	2015	2020	2020	2015	2020	2020	2015	2020
Total services	**175**	**124**	**-38.0**	**216**	**155**	**-30.7**	**-41**	**-31**
Transport	27	22	-26.3	59	45	-26.5	-33	-23
Travel	78	35	-63.0	54	18	-68.5	24	17
Others	70	67	-10.7	103	92	-12.2	-33	-25

Developing economies: Asia and Oceania

Service category	Exports			Imports			Balance	
	Value		Annual growth rate	Value		Annual growth rate		
	(Billions of US$)		(Percentage)	(Billions of US$)		(Percentage)	(Billions of US$)	
	2015	2020	2020	2015	2020	2020	2015	2020
Total services	**1 221**	**1 200**	**-23.6**	**1 511**	**1 344**	**-24.1**	**-290**	**-145**
Transport	273	265	-16.7	395	390	-16.6	-122	-126
Travel	366	145	-68.3	499	249	-55.9	-133	-104
Others	582	790	-0.7	617	705	-4.6	-35	85

Table 2.2.2 | **Exports of selected services, by region, 2020**
(Millions of United States dollars)

Group of economies	Insurance and pension services	Financial services	Charges for the use of intellectual property n.i.e.	Telecommunications, computer, and information services	Other business services
World	**143 475**	**539 567**	**390 541**	**710 431**	**1 338 009**
Northern America	22 216	154 443	119 796	66 464	212 980
Latin America and the Caribbean	6 042	5 224	1 118	9 671	30 046
Europe	80 901	281 091	192 028	402 589	688 037
Sub-Saharan Africa	1 116	2 326	262	2 820	10 899
Western Asia and Northern Africa	12 108	4 370	4 522	42 299	32 345
Central and Southern Asia	2 658	4 656	1 312	72 123	82 035
Eastern and South-Eastern Asia	17 925	83 699	69 818	109 548	272 270
Oceania	510	3 757	1 685	4 918	9 398
Selected groups					
Developing economies excluding China	32 180	78 686	24 061	148 356	289 641
Developing economies excluding LDCs	37 397	82 415	32 880	205 506	360 472
LDCs	233	538	60	1 884	4 616
LLDCs	415	478	-	2 382	3 360
SIDS (UN-OHRLLS)	14 374	33 683	8 335	17 263	65 278
HIPCs (IMF)	383	454	96	1 833	8 453
BRICS	9 036	11 113	12 029	136 256	180 206
G20	112 422	444 805	349 431	601 904	1 120 714

Economic trends

KEY FIGURES 2020

Change of world real
GDP per capita

-4.6%

FDI inflows to LDCs

US$24 billion

UNCTAD Commodity
Price Index

-16%

FORECAST 2021

World real GDP
growth

+5.3%

3.1 Gross domestic product

30 000 and more
8 000 to less than 30 000
3 000 to less than 8 000
1 000 to less than 3 000
0 to less than 1 000
No data

Concepts and definitions

GDP is an aggregate measure of production, income and expenditure of an economy. As a production measure, it represents the gross value added, i.e., the output net of intermediate consumption, achieved by all resident units engaged in production, plus any taxes less subsidies on products not included in the value of output. As an income measure, it represents the sum of primary incomes (gross wages and entrepreneurial income) distributed by resident producers, plus taxes less subsidies on production and imports. As an expenditure measure, it depicts the sum of expenditure on final consumption, gross capital formation (i.e., investment, changes in inventories, and acquisitions less disposals of valuables) and exports after deduction of imports (United Nations et al., 2009).

The GDP figures presented in this section are usually calculated from the expenditure side.

Trends in global economy

Global real GDP contracted by 3.6 per cent in 2020, and by 4.6 per cent measured per capita. Brought on by the COVID-19 pandemic, this annual decrease was three times bigger than that of 2009 following the global financial crisis. As the world economy recovers, GDP is forecast to expand by 5.3 per cent in 2021.

Large differences in GDP per capita persist throughout the world. In 2020, the median was represented by Belarus and Peru with just over US$6 000 in current prices. Most developed economies produced an output per person greater than US$30 000, with economies in Eastern Europe as the main exception. By contrast, 27 economies recorded a per capita output of less than US$1 000. Four out of ten economies in Africa were in this category together with Afghanistan, Haiti, Nepal, Tajikistan and Yemen.

Figure 3.1.1 | **World real gross domestic product, annual growth rate**
(Percentage)

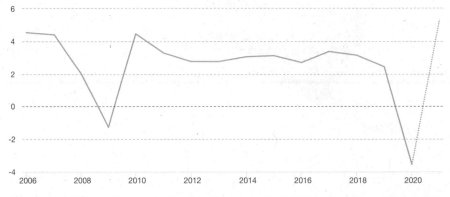

Note: In constant 2015 United States dollars. The dotted line indicates the UNCTAD forecast for the year 2021 (UNCTAD 2021b).

Regional trends

In 2020, GDP decreased more in developed than in developing economies. Only developing economies in America saw a more severe contraction than developed economies. As a result of continued economic growth in China, the contraction recorded for the developing economies in Asia and Oceania was only half a per cent. Excluding China, the growth rate of GDP was very similar for developing and developed economies.

The target of at least 7 per cent annual growth for LDCs set by the 2030 Agenda for Sustainable Development drifted further away from reach (United Nations, 2017). GDP in LDCs did not grow in 2020 and declined in per capita terms.

Figure 3.1.2 | **Growth of real gross domestic product by group of economies, 2020** (Percentage)

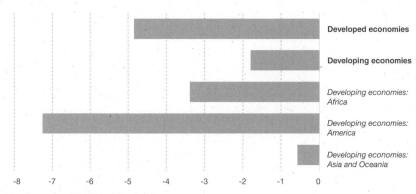

Note: In constant 2015 United States dollars.

Global economic inequality

Over the last 10 years, the global distribution of nominal GDP between economies has trended towards more equality. For example, in 2010, the poorest economies, accounting for 85 per cent of the world's population, contributed 34 per cent to world GDP. By 2020, their share in GDP was 38 per cent, even if the change from 2015 to 2020 was small. Still, half of the global population lived in an economy where GDP per capita was below US$4 000 in nominal terms in 2020. The figure is twenty times higher in Luxembourg, Bermuda, Switzerland, Liechtenstein, Cayman Islands and Ireland.

Figure 3.1.3 | **Distribution of world gross domestic product** (Percentage)

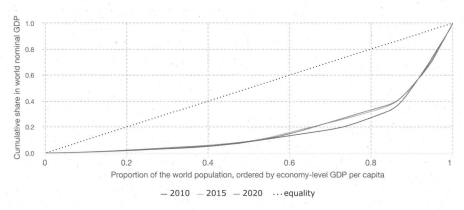

Note: Lorenz curves, as in this graph, reveal the structure of inequality. Inequality is greater the further the curve runs below the diagonal line (see annex 6.3). Inequality within economies is not considered.

World economy contracted

by 3.6% in 2020

World GDP growth forecast to be **5.3%** in 2021

GDP growth in LDCs still below

2030 Agenda target of 7%

The **richest** economies, accounting for **62%** of world **GDP** in 2020, host only **15%** of the world's population

Table 3.1.1 | Gross domestic product and gross domestic product per capita

Group of economies	Value		Annual growth rate			
	Nominal GDP	Nominal GDP per capita	Real GDP[a]		Real GDP[a] per capita	
	(Billions of US$)	(US$)	(Percentage)		(Percentage)	
	2020	2020	2019	2020	2019	2020
World	**84 884**	**10 892**	**2.4**	**-3.6**	**1.3**	**-4.6**
Developed economies	50 470	39 185	1.7	-4.8	1.4	-5.0
Developing economies	34 415	5 290	3.5	-1.8	2.3	-3.0
Developing economies: Africa	2 494	1 863	3.0	-3.4	0.5	-5.7
Developing economies: America	4 448	6 845	-0.6	-7.3	-1.5	-8.1
Developing economies: Asia and Oceania	27 473	6 082	4.4	-0.5	3.5	-1.4
Selected groups						
Developing economies excluding China	19 678	3 884	1.8	-4.6	0.3	-6.0
Developing economies excluding LDCs	33 260	6 105	3.5	-1.8	2.4	-2.8
LDCs	1 154	1 092	4.8	0.0	2.4	-2.3
LLDCs	924	1 733	4.3	-2.0	1.9	-4.2
SIDS (UN-OHRLLS)	723	10 630	1.8	-6.9	0.7	-7.9
HIPCs (IMF)	742	976	5.1	0.1	2.2	-2.6
BRICS	20 624	6 371	5.0	0.0	4.2	-0.6
G20	73 080	14 932	2.5	-3.4	1.9	-4.0

[a] In constant 2015 United States dollars.

Table 3.1.2 | Nominal gross domestic product by type of expenditure, 2019
(Percentage)

Group of economies	Final consumption		Gross capital formation	Net exports of goods and services
	Households[a]	Government[b]		
World	**56.4**	**16.6**	**26.3**	**0.7**
Developed economies	60.2	17.5	21.9	0.4
Developing economies	50.9	15.2	32.7	1.3
Developing economies: Africa	67.4	12.9	25.0	-5.0
Developing economies: America	66.3	16.2	18.6	-0.8
Developing economies: Asia and Oceania	46.5	15.2	36.1	2.3
Selected groups				
Developing economies excluding China	59.1	14.2	25.5	1.2
Developing economies excluding LDCs	50.4	15.3	32.8	1.6
LDCs	68.9	10.7	29.3	-8.4
LLDCs	60.8	12.6	29.8	-4.1
SIDS (UN-OHRLLS)	49.6	15.0	22.5	12.4
HIPCs (IMF)	69.6	12.0	27.3	-7.9
BRICS	45.5	16.4	37.0	1.3
G20	56.0	17.0	26.5	0.5

[a] Including non-profit institutions serving households.
[b] General government.

Table 3.1.3 | **Nominal gross value added by economic activity**
(Percentage)

Group of economies	Agriculture		Industry		Services	
	2009	2019	2009	2019	2009	2019
World	**3.8**	**4.2**	**28.0**	**27.9**	**68.1**	**67.9**
Developed economies	1.4	1.4	23.7	22.8	74.9	75.8
Developing economies	9.3	8.3	37.8	35.3	52.9	56.4
Developing economies: Africa	16.4	16.6	32.5	30.8	51.2	52.6
Developing economies: America	5.4	5.5	30.7	27.5	63.9	66.9
Developing economies: Asia and Oceania	9.6	8.1	40.7	37.1	49.7	54.8
Selected groups						
Developing economies excluding China	9.0	9.0	34.4	32.5	56.6	58.5
Developing economies excluding LDCs	8.8	7.9	38.1	35.5	53.1	56.6
LDCs	24.9	20.8	27.0	30.1	48.1	49.1
LLDCs	18.2	16.6	33.7	33.1	48.1	50.3
SIDS (UN-OHRLLS)	3.4	3.0	27.6	26.6	69.1	70.4
HIPCs (IMF)	26.3	23.7	25.5	27.9	48.2	48.4
BRICS	9.4	8.2	39.2	35.9	51.3	55.8
G20	3.1	3.5	27.1	27.3	69.8	69.2

Table 3.1.4 | **Economies with highest gross domestic product per capita**

Economy	Nominal value		Real annual growth rate[a]	Structure by type of expenditure			
				Final consumption		Gross capital formation	Net exports of goods and services
				Household[b]	Government[c]		
	(US$)		(Percentage)	(Percentage)	(Percentage)	(Percentage)	(Percentage)
	2019	2020	2020	2019	2019	2019	2019
Luxembourg	115 481	117 039	-2.9	29.5	17.1	17.4	36.0
Bermuda	117 764	108 161	-8.2	48.2	11.9	14.9	25.1
Switzerland, Liechtenstein	85 548	86 705	-3.7	52.0	11.2	24.5	12.3
Cayman Islands	92 694	85 134	-9.1	52.9	9.6	14.7	23.1
Ireland	81 637	84 941	1.4	29.3	11.9	46.0	12.3
Norway	74 985	66 420	-1.5	44.8	24.4	29.0	1.8
United States of America	64 854	63 000	-4.0	67.8	13.9	21.0	-2.8
Iceland	71 343	62 003	-7.2	50.8	24.3	20.1	4.7
Denmark	60 657	61 183	-3.0	46.1	23.8	22.7	7.4
Singapore	64 103	57 754	-6.1	36.0	10.3	24.9	27.9

Note: Economies are ranked by the nominal value in 2020.
[a] In constant 2015 United States dollars.
[b] Including non-profit institutions serving households.
[c] General government.

3.2 Current account

Map 3.2 | **Current account balance as a ratio to gross domestic product, 2020**
(Percentage)

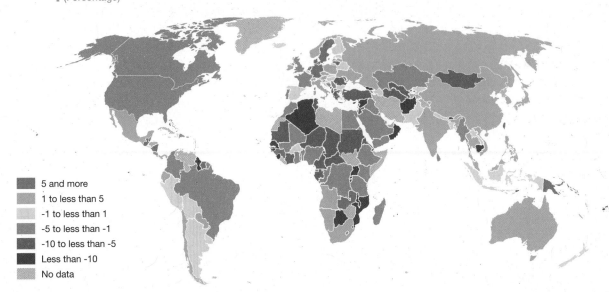

- 5 and more
- 1 to less than 5
- -1 to less than 1
- -5 to less than -1
- -10 to less than -5
- Less than -10
- No data

Concepts and definitions

The current account, within the balance of payments, displays the transactions between residents and non-residents of a reporting economy, involving economic values, namely the cross-national exchange of goods and services as well as cross-national transfers of primary and secondary income.

The current account balance shows the difference between the sum of exports and income receivable, and the sum of imports and income payable, where exports and imports refer to both goods and services, while income refers to both primary and secondary income. A surplus in the current account is recorded when receipts exceed payments; a deficit is recorded when payments exceed receipts.

The current account data in this section correspond to the latest reporting standard, known as BPM6, defined by the International Monetary Fund (2009).

Current account imbalances across the world

Receipts earned by economies from transactions with other economies often differ significantly from the payments made. In 2020, for most economies in America, Africa, South-Eastern Europe, and Central and Western Asia, payments exceeded receipts, leading to negative current account balances. Higher surpluses were found mainly in Central, Northern and Eastern Europe, Eastern Asia, and Oceania. Most economies in the South of African continent also achieved positive current account balances.

Figure 3.2.1 | **Balances in the current account**
(Billions of United States dollars)

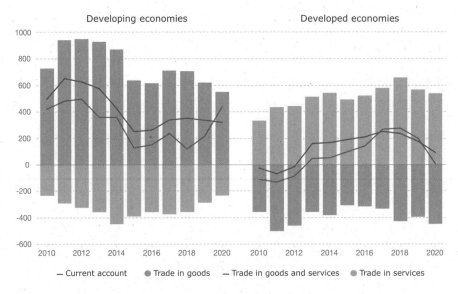

— Current account   ● Trade in goods   — Trade in goods and services   ● Trade in services

Note: Current account deficits and surpluses do not add up to zero at the world level, due to imperfect geographic coverage and cross-country differences in compilation methods.

In 2020, Kuwait recorded the highest current account surplus relative to GDP (30 per cent). Tuvalu, Guinea, and Papua New Guinea enjoyed surpluses close to 20 per cent of their respective GDP.

In absolute terms, the United States of America (US$616 billion) and the United Kingdom (US$95 billion) ran the world's largest current account deficits. China (US$274 billion) had the largest absolute surplus, followed by Germany (US$266 billion) and Japan (US$164 billion).

Recent developments

In 2020, the current account surplus of developing economies doubled (US$438 billion) compared with 2019 (US$213 billion), although their surplus of trade in goods and services showed a slight decrease (from US$335 million to US$317 million). Geographically, the increase in the current account balance can largely be attributed to a growing surplus in developing economies of Asia and Oceania (from US$406 billion to US$531 billion), combined with a shrinking deficit in developing economies in America (from US$102 billion to US$2 billion). The current account surplus of developed economies fell to only US$5 billion in 2020, from US$197 billion recorded for the year before.

Figure 3.2.2 | **Balances in least developed countries' current accounts**
(Billions of United States dollars)

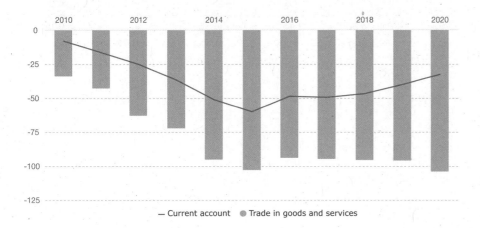

— Current account   ● Trade in goods and services

Least developed countries keep lowering their deficit

After five years of continuous decline, the current account balance of LDCs shows an increasing trend since 2015, resulting in a reduction of their deficit by almost a half, from US$60 billion to US$33 billion. The trade deficit has nevertheless remained at around US$100 billion.

Greater relative current account deficit, accounting for 2.9 per cent of GDP in 2020, distinguishes LDCs from other developing economies, which, as a group, ran a surplus of 1.3 per cent of GDP. Higher deficits relative to GDP were registered for the groups of heavily indebted poor countries (HIPCs) (4.2 per cent) and landlocked developing countries (LLDCs) (3.2 per cent). As a group, small island developing States (SIDS) registered a comfortable 7 per cent surplus. Yet, some SIDS faced deficits close to, or over, 20 per cent of GDP.

Current account deficit larger than $\frac{1}{5}$ **of GDP** **in several SIDS**

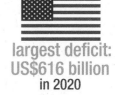

United States of America keeps having world's **largest deficit: US$616 billion in 2020**

Developing economies' surplus doubled in 2020, almost returning to 2012 levels

LDCs' deficit shrinking for the fifth consecutive year. **US$33 billion in 2020**

Table 3.2.1 | Current account balance by group of economies

Group of economies	Value (Billions of US$)			Ratio to GDP (Percentage)		
	2016–2020[a]	2019	2020	2016–2020[a]	2019	2020
World	**406**	**410**	**443**	**0.5**	**0.5**	**0.5**
Developed economies	176	197	5	0.4	0.4	0.0
Developing economies	230	213	438	0.7	0.6	1.3
Developing economies: Africa	-88	-91	-91	-3.8	-3.7	-3.7
Developing economies: America	-87	-102	-2	-1.6	-1.9	-0.1
Developing economies: Asia and Oceania	405	406	531	1.6	1.5	1.9
Selected groups						
Developing economies excluding China	74	110	164	0.4	0.5	0.8
Developing economies excluding LDCs	274	253	470	0.8	0.7	1.4
LDCs	-43	-40	-33	-4.1	-3.7	-2.9
LLDCs	-32	-36	-29	-4.1	-4.4	-3.2
SIDS (UN-OHRLLS)	55	53	49	7.5	6.8	7.0
HIPCs (IMF)	-38	-36	-31	-5.6	-4.9	-4.2
BRICS	144	63	324	0.7	0.3	1.6
G20	223	204	283	0.3	0.3	0.4

Note: Current account deficits and surpluses do not add up to zero at the world level, due to imperfect geographic coverage and cross-country differences in compilation methods.
[a] Annual average.

Table 3.2.2 | Current account balance in largest surplus and deficit economies

Economy (Ranked by 2020 value)	2016–2020[a]		2019		2020	
	Value (Billions of US$)	Ratio to GDP (Percentage)	Value (Billions of US$)	Ratio to GDP (Percentage)	Value (Billions of US$)	Ratio to GDP (Percentage)
China	156	1.2	103	0.7	274	1.9
Germany	290	7.8	290	7.5	266	7.0
Japan	184	3.7	177	3.5	164	3.3
China, Taiwan Province of	77	12.8	65	10.7	95	14.2
Korea, Republic of	77	4.8	60	3.6	75	4.6
⋮	⋮	⋮	⋮	⋮	⋮	⋮
Canada	-40	-2.4	-36	-2.0	-30	-1.8
Turkey	-24	-3.0	7	0.9	-37	-5.2
France	-21	-0.8	-8	-0.3	-50	-1.9
United Kingdom	-107	-3.9	-88	-3.1	-95	-3.5
United States of America	-457	-2.2	-472	-2.2	-616	-2.9

[a] Annual average.

Table 3.2.3 | Current accounts of leading exporters (goods and services) by group of economies, 2020

Developed economies

Economy (Ranked by export share)	Current account balance		Trade balance[a]	Exports[a]	Imports[a]
	Value (Billions of US$)	Ratio to GDP (Percentage)	Value (Billions of US$)	Share in world (Percentage)	Share in world (Percentage)
United States of America	-616	-2.9	-670	9.7	13.0
Germany	266	7.0	218	7.6	6.7
Japan	164	3.3	(e) 4	(e) 3.6	(e) 3.6
France	-50	-1.9	-58	3.4	3.7
United Kingdom	-95	-3.5	-10	3.4	3.5
Developed economies	**5**	**0.0**	**89**	**58.3**	**59.0**

[a] Goods and services.

Developing economies

Economy (Ranked by export share)	Current account balance		Trade balance[a]	Exports[a]	Imports[a]
	Value	Ratio to GDP	Value	Share in world	Share in world
	(Billions of US$)	(Percentage)	(Billions of US$)	(Percentage)	(Percentage)
China	274	1.9	415	12.6	10.9
Korea, Republic of	75	4.6	(e) 66	(e) 2.7	(e) 2.5
China, Hong Kong SAR	23	6.5	-31	2.6	2.8
Singapore	60	17.7	60	2.6	2.3
India	33	1.2	(e) -45	2.2	(e) 2.4
Developing economies	**438**	**1.3**	**317**	**41.7**	**41.0**

[a] Goods and services.

Developing economies: Africa

Economy (Ranked by export share)	Current account balance		Trade balance[a]	Exports[a]	Imports[a]
	Value	Ratio to GDP	Value	Share in world	Share in world
	(Billions of US$)	(Percentage)	(Billions of US$)	(Percentage)	(Percentage)
South Africa	7	2.2	15	0.4	0.4
Egypt	-14	-4.0	-32	0.2	0.3
Nigeria	-17	-4.0	-32	0.2	0.3
Morocco	-2	-1.4	-9	0.2	0.2
Algeria	-18	-12.9	(e) -19	(e) 0.1	(e) 0.2
Developing Africa	**-91**	**-3.7**	**-176**	**2.1**	**2.9**

[a] Goods and services.

Developing economies: America

Economy (Ranked by export share)	Current account balance		Trade balance[a]	Exports[a]	Imports[a]
	Value	Ratio to GDP	Value	Share in world	Share in world
	(Billions of US$)	(Percentage)	(Billions of US$)	(Percentage)	(Percentage)
Mexico	26	2.4	(e) 26	(e) 2.0	(e) 1.9
Brazil	-26	-1.8	12	1.1	1.1
Chile	3	1.3	13	0.4	0.3
Argentina	3	0.8	12	0.3	0.2
Peru	(e) 2	(e) 0.8	(e) 4	(e) 0.2	(e) 0.2
Developing America	**-2**	**-0.1**	**18**	**4.9**	**4.9**

[a] Goods and services.

Developing economies: Asia and Oceania

Economy (Ranked by export share)	Current account balance		Trade balance[a]	Exports[a]	Imports[a]
	Value	Ratio to GDP	Value	Share in world	Share in world
	(Billions of US$)	(Percentage)	(Billions of US$)	(Percentage)	(Percentage)
China	274	1.9	415	12.6	10.9
Korea, Republic of	75	4.6	(e) 66	(e) 2.7	(e) 2.5
China, Hong Kong SAR	23	6.5	-31	2.6	2.8
Singapore	60	17.7	60	2.6	2.3
India	33	1.2	(e) -45	2.2	(e) 2.4
Developing Asia and Oceania	**531**	**1.9**	**475**	**34.7**	**33.2**

[a] Goods and services.

3.3 Foreign direct investment

Map 3.3 | Foreign direct investment inflows as a ratio to gross domestic product, 2020

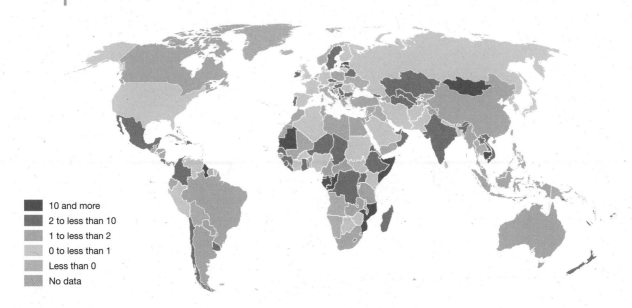

- 10 and more
- 2 to less than 10
- 1 to less than 2
- 0 to less than 1
- Less than 0
- No data

Concepts and definitions

Foreign direct investment (FDI) is defined as an investment reflecting a lasting interest and control by a foreign direct investor, resident in one economy, in an enterprise resident in another economy (foreign affiliate).

FDI inflows comprise capital provided by a foreign direct investor to a foreign affiliate, or capital received by a foreign direct investor from a foreign affiliate. FDI outflows represent the same flows from the perspective of the other economy.

FDI flows are presented on a net basis, i.e., as credits less debits. Thus, in cases of reverse investment or disinvestment, FDI may be negative.

FDI stock is the value of capital and reserves attributable to a non-resident parent enterprise, plus the net indebtedness of foreign affiliates to parent enterprises (UNCTAD, 2021c).

Trends and global patterns

FDI fell dramatically in 2020 during the COVID-19 crisis. Global FDI flows dropped by 35 per cent in 2020, to US$1.0 trillion from US$1.5 trillion in 2019. This is almost 20 per cent below the 2009 financial crisis level.

The decline was heavily skewed towards developed economies, where FDI inflows fell sharply by 59 per cent to US$329 billion in 2020, a level last seen in 2003. FDI flows to Europe fell by 78 per cent, largely because of negative FDI in countries with significant conduit flows, such as the Netherlands and Switzerland. FDI to North America declined somewhat less sharply, by 42 per cent.

FDI to developing economies decreased at a more moderate 9 per cent rate, mainly because of robust flows in Asia. The fall in FDI flows across developing regions was uneven, with 45 per cent in America and 16 per cent in Africa. In contrast, flows to Asia rose by 3 per cent.

Figure 3.3.1 | **World foreign direct investment inflows** (Billions of United States dollars)

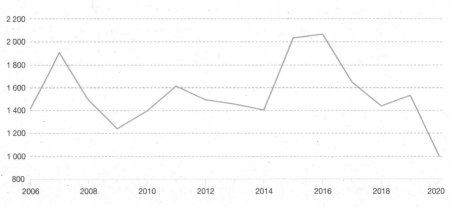

Note: Excluding financial centres in the Caribbean (see note, table 3.3.1).

Inflows and outflows by group of economies

In 2020, FDI from developed economies decreased by 56 per cent to US$354 billion, the lowest since 1997. Outflows from Europe (including large negative flows) fell by 79 per cent to US$80 billion. Outflows from developing countries fell by 7 per cent to US$386 billion. Developing Asia was the only region recording expansion in outflows, increasing by 6 per cent to US$388 billion. FDI outflows from Africa fell by 68 per cent in 2020 to US$1.6 billion from US$4.9 billion in 2019. Outflows from developing America collapsed in 2020, recording an overall disinvestment for the first time ever (-US$3.5 billion).

Figure 3.3.2 | Foreign direct investment inflows and outflows, 2020
(Billions of United States dollars)

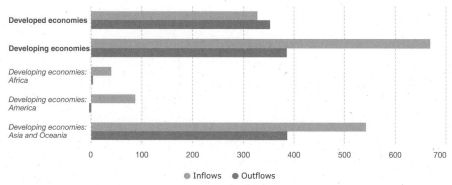

● Inflows   ● Outflows

Note: Excluding financial centres in the Caribbean (see note, table 3.3.1).

Origins and destinations of foreign direct investment

Developed economies' share in global outward FDI dropped to a record low of 48 per cent in 2020. Europe accounted for 11 per cent, North America accounted for 19 per cent and developed Asia accounted for 16 per cent.

On the recipient side, as a result of robust flows in Asia, developing economies accounted for 67 per cent of global FDI inflows, up from 48 per cent in 2019. Developing Asia is the only region recording growth, accounting for 54 per cent of global inward flows. Developing America accounts for 9 per cent and Africa for 4 per cent.[1]

[1] For further analyses on that topic, see UNCTAD (2021c).

Figure 3.3.3 | Selected foreign direct investment flows
(Percentage of world total)

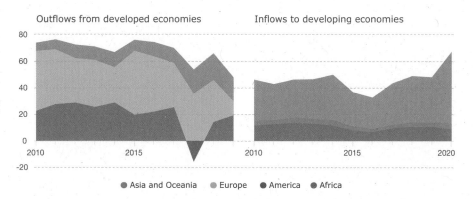

● Asia and Oceania   ● Europe   ● America   ● Africa

Note: Excluding financial centres in the Caribbean (see note, table 3.3.1).

Global **FDI inflows** fell sharply **by 35%** in 2020

In 2020, FDI from developed economies decreased by 56%, the lowest level since 1997

Developing Asia  accounted for 54% of global inflows

Asia and Oceania remained the largest FDI recipient of the developing regions

Table 3.3.1 | **Foreign direct investment flows by group of economies**

Group of economies	Inflows				Outflows			
	Value (Billions of US$)		Ratio to GDP (Percentage)		Value (Billions of US$)		Ratio to GDP (Percentage)	
	2019	2020	2019	2020	2019	2020	2019	2020
World[a]	**1 530**	**999**	**1.8**	**1.2**	**1 220**	**740**	**1.4**	**0.9**
Developed economies	796	329	1.5	0.7	804	354	1.5	0.7
Developing economies	734	670	2.1	2.0	417	386	1.2	1.2
Developing economies: Africa	47	40	1.9	1.6	5	2	0.2	0.1
Developing economies: America	160	88	3.1	2.0	47	-4	1.0	-0.1
Developing economies: Asia and Oceania	527	543	1.9	2.0	365	388	1.3	1.4
Selected groups								
Developing economies excluding China	593	521	2.8	2.7	280	253	1.4	1.4
Developing economies excluding LDCs	711	647	2.1	2.0	418	383	1.2	1.2
LDCs	23	24	2.1	2.1	-1	3	-0.1	0.4
LLDCs	22	15	2.7	1.7	1	-1	0.1	-0.1
SIDS (UN-OHRLLS)	123	97	19.2	16.6	51	34	9.6	6.9
HIPCs (IMF)	28	23	3.8	3.1	2	3	0.4	0.5
BRICS	294	251	1.4	1.2	194	123	0.9	0.6
G20	1 171	659	1.6	0.9	1 072	500	1.4	0.7

Note: Excluding financial centres in the Caribbean, namely: Anguilla, Antigua and Barbuda, Aruba, the Bahamas, Barbados, British Virgin Islands, Cayman Islands, Curaçao, Dominica, Grenada, Montserrat, Saint Kitts and Nevis, Saint Lucia, Saint Vincent and the Grenadines, Sint Maarten and Turks and Caicos Islands.
[a] At world level, recorded FDI inflows may not equal recorded FDI outflows, due to imperfect geographic coverage and cross-country differences in compilation methods.

Table 3.3.2 | **Foreign direct investment stock by group of economies**

Group of economies	Inward stock				Outward stock			
	Value (Billions of US$)		Ratio to GDP (Percentage)		Value (Billions of US$)		Ratio to GDP (Percentage)	
	2019	2020	2019	2020	2019	2020	2019	2020
World[a]	**36 377**	**41 354**	**41.7**	**48.8**	**34 350**	**39 246**	**39.7**	**46.7**
Developed economies	24 766	29 285	47.6	58.0	26 264	30 526	50.5	60.5
Developing economies	11 611	12 069	32.9	35.2	8 086	8 720	23.4	26.0
Developing economies: Africa	942	979	38.4	39.3	289	326	13.0	14.7
Developing economies: America	2 260	2 232	43.6	51.8	729	771	14.8	18.8
Developing economies: Asia and Oceania	8 410	8 858	30.4	32.2	7 068	7 623	25.8	28.0
Selected groups								
Developing economies excluding China	9 842	10 150	47.0	52.0	5 887	6 368	29.1	33.8
Developing economies excluding LDCs	11 240	11 673	32.9	35.2	8 065	8 696	23.8	26.5
LDCs	371	395	34.2	34.4	21	24	2.9	3.2
LLDCs	408	418	49.1	45.5	50	50	8.4	7.3
SIDS (UN-OHRLLS)	1 911	2 023	296.4	345.7	1 128	1 246	208.7	253.5
HIPCs (IMF)	349	374	47.6	50.5	23	26	4.2	4.7
BRICS	3 540	3 591	16.8	17.4	3 249	3 450	15.4	16.7
G20	27 320	31 938	36.3	43.7	28 187	32 605	37.4	44.6

Note: Excluding financial centres in the Caribbean (see note, table 3.3.1).
[a] At world level, recorded inward stocks may not equal recorded outward stocks, due to imperfect geographic coverage and cross-country differences in compilation methods.

Table 3.3.3 | **Foreign direct investment inflows, top 20 host economies, 2020**

Economy (Ranked by inflow value)	Inflows		Inward stock
	Value	Ratio to GDP	Ratio to GDP
	(Billions of US$)	(Percentage)	(Percentage)
United States of America	156	0.7	51.3
China	149	1.0	13.0
China, Hong Kong SAR	119	34.1	539.1
Singapore	91	26.8	549.1
India	64	2.4	17.9
Luxembourg	62	84.8	856.3
Germany	36	0.9	27.9
Ireland	33	8.0	321.9
Mexico	29	2.7	56.0
Sweden	26	4.9	76.1
Brazil	25	1.7	42.8
Israel	25	6.1	46.9
Canada	24	1.4	66.9
Australia	20	1.5	58.8
United Arab Emirates	20	5.6	42.3
United Kingdom	20	0.7	81.5
Indonesia	19	1.8	22.7
France	18	0.7	37.2
Viet Nam	16	5.9	65.8
Japan	10	0.2	4.9

Note: Excluding financial centres in the Caribbean (see note, table 3.3.1).

Table 3.3.4 | **Foreign direct investment outflows, top 20 home economies, 2020**

Economy (Ranked by outflow value)	Outflows		Outward stock
	Value	Ratio to GDP	Ratio to GDP
	(Billions of US$)	(Percentage)	(Percentage)
China	133	0.9	16.0
Luxembourg	127	173.5	1 210.7
Japan	116	2.3	39.8
China, Hong Kong SAR	102	29.2	558.9
United States of America	93	0.4	38.6
Canada	49	3.0	119.5
France	44	1.7	66.1
Germany	35	0.9	52.2
Korea, Republic of	32	2.0	30.7
Singapore	32	9.6	361.3
Sweden	31	5.8	86.5
Spain	21	1.7	48.8
United Arab Emirates	19	5.3	57.1
Switzerland, Liechtenstein	17	2.2	216.1
Thailand	17	3.3	31.1
China, Taiwan Province of	14	2.1	57.3
Chile	12	4.5	56.9
India	12	0.4	7.1
Italy	10	0.5	31.6
Belgium	10	2.0	131.8

Note: Excluding financial centres in the Caribbean (see note, table 3.3.1).

3.4 Prices

Map 3.4 | **Annual growth of consumer prices, 2020**
(Percentage)

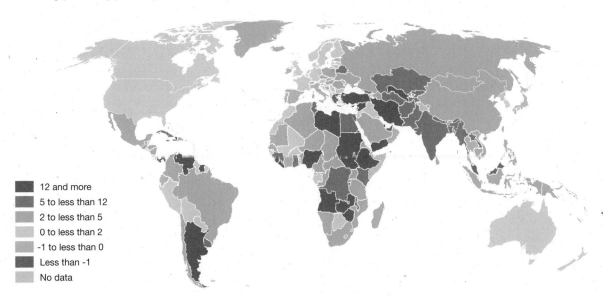

- 12 and more
- 5 to less than 12
- 2 to less than 5
- 0 to less than 2
- -1 to less than 0
- Less than -1
- No data

Concepts and definitions

Changes in consumer prices are measured by the consumer price index (CPI), which depicts the price of a basket of consumer goods and services representing average consumption by private households during a year, relative to the base year 2010.

The UNCTAD Commodity Price Index (UCPI) measures the average price, in United States dollars, of main primary commodities exported by developing economies relative to the base year 2015. The weights used in the calculation of the average price represent the shares of commodity groups in developing economies' total commodity exports observed over three years from 2014 to 2016. The overall index is decomposed into sub-indices displaying the price movements of individual commodity groups. The basket of the UCPI was entirely overhauled in 2018. For details, see annex 6.3 and UNCTAD (2018).

Growth of consumer prices worldwide

Inflation rates varied widely across the world's economies in 2020. Consumer prices increased relatively quickly in several economies across developing regions. They grew by around 2 400 per cent in Venezuela and 560 per cent in Zimbabwe. Inflation rates above 80 per cent were also recorded in the Sudan, the Syrian Arab Republic and Lebanon. In most economies, growth of consumer prices was between 0 and 5 per cent, but one in six economies - most of them relatively small in area - experienced price decreases in 2020.

Trends in exchange rates

Exchange rates of the most traded currencies remained relatively stable over the last four years. From 2019 to 2020, the yen and the euro appreciated by around 2 per cent against the United States dollar, the yuan and the pound sterling. Over the last decade, the dollar has appreciated against all four other currencies mentioned.

Figure 3.4.1 | **Exchange rates against the United States dollar**
(Annual average)

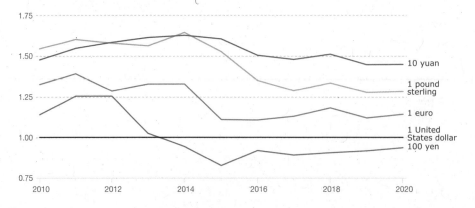

Commodity price index fell, led by fuel prices

On an annual basis, the UCPI was 16 per cent lower in 2020 compared to 2019. Excluding fuels, however, the index was up by 11 per cent. Fuels make up a large part of the index and their prices declined by 32 per cent from 2019. Prices also decreased for agricultural raw materials, but with a comparatively modest 2 per cent. The impact on the overall index was offset by a 6 per cent increase in food prices and a 16 per cent increase in the prices of minerals, ores and metals.

Figure 3.4.2 | **UNCTAD Commodity Price Index**
(2015=100)

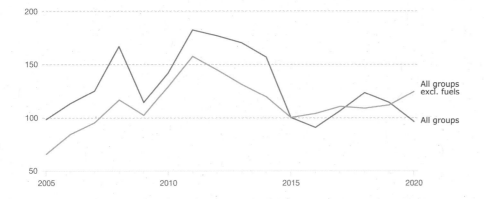

Commodity prices surged starting May 2020

The year 2020 saw both a sharp drop and a subsequent strong recovery of commodity prices. With the outbreak of the COVID-19 pandemic, prices began tumbling, and the UCPI reached a five-year low in April 2020. Fuel prices were at less than half of their level in the same month of the previous year. Agricultural raw material prices decreased by 11 per cent from April 2019 to April 2020, while food prices and prices for minerals, ores and metals recorded growth.

In April 2021, commodity prices surpassed pre-pandemic levels. Much as they drove the UCPI's initial downturn in 2020, significant changes in fuel prices drove its recovery as well. By April 2021, fuel prices had risen by 143 per cent year-on-year. As the prices for other commodities increased more modestly, albeit consistently, prices for all major groups were higher than twelve months earlier.

Figure 3.4.3 | **Year-on-year growth of prices by commodity group**
(Percentage)

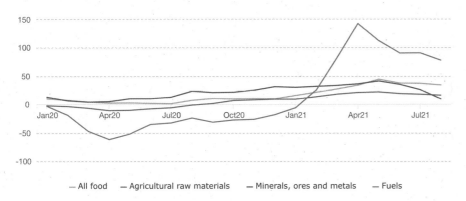

— All food   — Agricultural raw materials   — Minerals, ores and metals   — Fuels

Note: Percentage change of UCPI sub-indices, compared to the same month in the previous year.

Deflation in one out of six economies in 2020

Yen and euro appreciated by 2% against United States dollar, yuan and pound sterling

Commodity prices at a five-year low in April 2020, thereafter **sharp recovery**

In April 2021, fuel prices 143% above April 2020 levels

Table 3.4.1 | Consumer prices by group of economies

Group of economies	Consumer price index (2010=100)		Annual growth rate[a] (Percentage)	
	2015	2020	2015–2020	2020
World	**116**	**133**	**2.9**	**2.8**
Developed economies	109	118	1.6	0.9
Developing economies	128	161	4.7	5.4
Developing economies: Africa	148	274	12.9	17.8
Developing economies: America	137	200	7.9	7.7
Developing economies: Asia and Oceania	123	145	3.3	3.7
Selected groups				
Developing economies excluding China	135	184	6.4	7.4
Developing economies excluding LDCs	127	157	4.4	4.8
LDCs	161	323	14.4	22.4
LLDCs	141	249	11.3	20.3
SIDS (UN-OHRLLS)	118	131	2.1	2.1
HIPCs (IMF)	140	191	6.4	7.2
BRICS	125	144	2.9	3.1
G20	114	128	2.4	2.1

[a] Least squares growth rate (see annex 6.3)
Note: Venezuela is not considered.

Table 3.4.2 | Exchange rate and consumer prices among main exporting economies

Economy (Ranked by share in world exports)	Exchange rate to United States dollar			Consumer price index (2010=100)			Share in world exports[a] (Percentage)
	2018	2019	2020	2018	2019	2020	2020
China	0.15115	0.14475	0.14491	121	125	128	12.6
United States of America	1.00000	1.00000	1.00000	115	117	119	9.7
Germany	1.18095	1.11947	1.14220	112	114	114	7.6
Japan	0.00906	0.00917	0.00937	105	105	105	(e) 3.6
France	1.18095	1.11947	1.14220	110	112	112	3.4
United Kingdom	1.33417	1.27641	1.28205	118	121	122	3.4
Netherlands	1.18095	1.11947	1.14220	112	115	116	3.3
Korea, Republic of	0.00091	0.00086	0.00085	115	115	116	(e) 2.7
China, Hong Kong SAR	0.12758	0.12762	0.12891	131	135	135	2.6
Singapore	0.74138	0.73305	0.72477	114	114	114	2.6
Italy	1.18095	1.11947	1.14220	111	111	111	2.5
Ireland	1.18095	1.11947	1.14220	105	106	105	2.4
India	0.01462	0.01420	0.01350	164	172	182	2.2
Canada	0.77171	0.75370	0.74563	115	117	118	(e) 2.2
Switzerland, Liechtenstein	1.02262	1.00626	1.06514	99	100	99	2.1
Mexico	0.05196	0.05191	0.04654	137	142	146	(e) 2.0
Belgium	1.18095	1.11947	1.14220	116	117	118	1.9
Spain	1.18095	1.11947	1.14220	110	111	111	1.8
Russian Federation	0.01596	0.01545	0.01387	173	181	187	(e) 1.7
China, Taiwan Province of	0.03315	0.03233	0.03380	109	109	109	1.6

[a] Exports of goods and services.

Table 3.4.3 | **Price indices of selected primary commodities**
(2015=100)

Commodity group	2010	2011	2012	2013	2014	2015	2016	2017	2018	2019	2020
All groups	**142**	**182**	**177**	**170**	**157**	**100**	**91**	**106**	**123**	**114**	**96**
All food	114	141	132	120	119	100	104	102	96	94	100
Food	111	135	127	120	118	100	104	103	96	98	102
Tropical beverages	110	144	112	90	111	100	97	94	86	81	85
Vegetable oilseeds and oils	121	151	152	136	123	100	107	106	100	93	106
Agricultural raw materials	142	177	143	131	115	100	100	105	103	99	97
Minerals, ores and metals	136	164	153	138	121	100	105	116	118	125	145
Minerals, ores and non-precious metals	170	191	159	156	133	100	101	128	131	135	140
Precious metals	110	143	148	125	111	100	107	108	108	117	148
Fuels	150	198	197	194	180	100	83	104	133	116	79
Selected groups											
Tropical beverages and food	111	137	124	112	117	100	102	101	94	94	98
All groups excl. fuels	129	158	145	131	119	100	104	110	109	112	124
All groups excl. precious metals	146	188	181	176	163	100	88	106	126	114	89
All groups excl. precious metals and fuels	138	164	143	134	123	100	102	112	109	109	114

Table 3.4.4 | **Monthly price indices of main commodity groups**
(2015=100)

	Period	All groups	All food	Agricultural raw materials	Minerals, ores and metals	Fuels
2020	January	**114**	102	99	132	112
	February	**104**	100	97	130	97
	March	**83**	96	94	127	65
	April	**73**	94	91	129	49
	May	**81**	93	91	134	60
	June	**90**	95	92	139	72
	July	**95**	96	93	148	76
	August	**100**	99	96	159	81
	September	**98**	102	98	158	77
	October	**99**	103	103	156	78
	November	**103**	109	104	157	83
	December	**113**	112	107	167	95
2021	January	**121**	118	108	171	105
	February	**132**	121	110	171	122
	March	**130**	122	112	169	119
	April	**132**	126	110	175	119
	May	**141**	134	110	189	128
	June	**147**	131	110	188	138
	July	**151**	131	109	186	145
	August	**148**	133	111	174	144

4

Population

KEY FIGURES **2020**

World population
7.8 billion

Annual
population growth
+1.0%

Share of urban
population in
developing economies
52%

Child dependency
ratio in LDCs
67%

4.1 Total and urban population

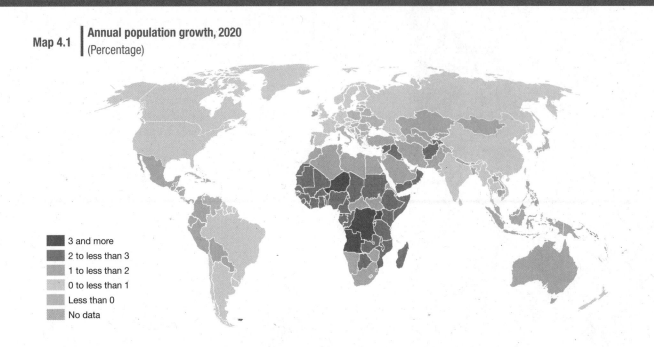

Map 4.1 | **Annual population growth, 2020**
(Percentage)

- 3 and more
- 2 to less than 3
- 1 to less than 2
- 0 to less than 1
- Less than 0
- No data

Concepts and definitions

The population estimates and projections reported in this chapter represent the population present in an economy (including residents, migrants and refugees) as of 1 July of a given year (UN DESA, 2019a, 2019b).

The figures for the years from 2020 to 2050 are based on the medium fertility variant projection. The assumptions for these projections imply that the average fertility rate of the world will decline from 2.5 births per woman in 2019 to 2.2 in 2050. The United Nations also produce other projection variants. Their outcome is highly dependent on the path that future fertility takes (UN DESA, 2019b). Projections were made in 2019 and the effects of the COVID-19 pandemic are currently unknown (UN DESA, 2021).

Urban population is defined as the population living in areas classified as urban according to the criteria used by each country or territory (UN DESA, 2018, 2019c).

Slowdown of world population growth

The steady slowdown in world population growth, taking place since the late 1980s, continued in 2020. According to projections from 2019, not considering the outbreak of COVID-19, world population grew by 1.0 per cent in 2020, or 81 million people, to reach a global total of 7.8 billion. In the coming decades, the slowdown in the rate of population growth is projected to continue. By 2050, it is forecast to fall below 0.5 per cent per year.

The population of Africa is growing especially fast. In 2020, with a rate of 2.5 per cent, it increased at more than double the pace of the world total. Several economies in Sub-Saharan Africa recorded growth rates well above 3 per cent. Rates higher than the global average were also common in Western, Southern and South-Eastern Asia and in parts of South America. Developed economies experienced generally low population growth, 0.2 per cent on average. In 2020, population was expected to have declined in several Eastern and Southern European economies, as well as, for example, Venezuela, Cuba, Georgia and Japan.

Figure 4.1.1 | **Annual growth rate of world population**
(Percentage)

Developing economies drive population growth

Over the last 30 years, the world population has increased by 2.5 billion people. Most of this growth occurred in developing economies, mainly in Asia and Oceania. Today, 84 per cent of the world's population live in a developing economy. In 1990, this figure was only 77 per cent.

In the next 30 years, global population is projected to grow by 1.9 billion people. The population of the developing world will continue to grow. The population of Africa alone is projected to grow by 1.1 billion. One quarter of the world population will live in Africa, as compared to one sixth today.

Figure 4.1.2 | **World population by group of economies** (Billions)

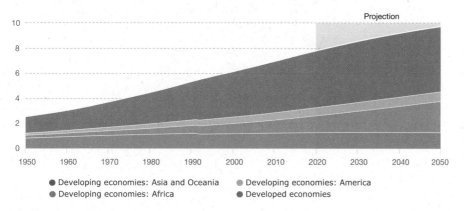

- Developing economies: Asia and Oceania
- Developing economies: America
- Developing economies: Africa
- Developed economies

Urbanization continues

All over the world, a growing proportion of the population lives in cities. In 2010, 51.6 per cent lived in urban areas. By 2020, the share of urban population increased to 56.2 per cent. It is generally higher in the developed (79.2 per cent in 2020) than in the developing world (51.6 per cent). In LDCs, the people living in urban areas are in the minority (34.6 per cent).

Over the last ten years, urbanization has been most pronounced in developing economies, especially in Asia and Oceania, which saw the urbanization rate increase from 43.1 in 2010 to 49.8 per cent in 2020. By contrast, further urbanization in the developing economies of America has been relatively modest. Urbanization levels in this region are already comparable to developed economies.

Figure 4.1.3 | **Urban population by group of economies** (Percentage of total population)

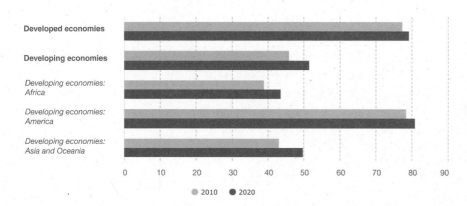

● 2010 ● 2020

World population has **increased by 2.5 billion people** in the **last 30 years**

Population of **Africa growing** at more than **double the pace** of the world average: **2.5% per year**

By 2050, an additional 2 billion people will live on earth

In **developed economies, 79%** of people live in cities

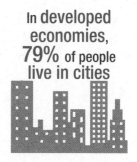

Table 4.1.1 | Total population by group of economies

Group of economies	Population (Millions)			Annual growth rate[a] (Percentage)		
	2015	2020	2050	2015–2020	2020	2020–2050
World	**7 380**	**7 795**	**9 735**	**1.1**	**1.0**	**0.7**
Developed economies	1 271	1 288	1 299	0.3	0.2	0.0
Developing economies	6 108	6 506	8 436	1.3	1.2	0.9
Developing economies: Africa	1 181	1 339	2 488	2.5	2.5	2.1
Developing economies: America	619	650	759	1.0	0.9	0.5
Developing economies: Asia and Oceania	4 308	4 517	5 189	0.9	0.9	0.5
Selected groups						
Developing economies excluding China	4 702	5 067	7 033	1.5	1.5	1.1
Developing economies excluding LDCs	5 168	5 449	6 560	1.1	1.0	0.6
LDCs	941	1 057	1 876	2.3	2.3	1.9
LLDCs	474	533	926	2.4	2.3	1.8
SIDS (UN-OHRLLS)	65	68	84	1.1	1.1	0.7
HIPCs (IMF)	662	760	1 482	2.8	2.7	2.2
BRICS	3 122	3 237	3 482	0.7	0.7	0.2
G20	4 729	4 894	5 277	0.7	0.6	0.3

[a] Exponential growth rate (see annex 6.3).

Table 4.1.2 | Urban population by group of economies

Group of economies	Urban population (Millions)			Share in total population (Percentage)		
	2015	2020	2050	2015	2020	2050
World	**3 980**	**4 380**	**6 656**	**53.9**	**56.2**	**68.4**
Developed economies	995	1 020	1 125	78.3	79.2	86.6
Developing economies	2 985	3 359	5 531	48.9	51.6	65.6
Developing economies: Africa	487	583	1 470	41.2	43.5	59.1
Developing economies: America	494	526	665	79.8	81.0	87.7
Developing economies: Asia and Oceania	2 004	2 250	3 396	46.5	49.8	65.4
Selected groups						
Developing economies excluding China	2 204	2 475	4 408	46.9	48.8	62.7
Developing economies excluding LDCs	2 684	2 993	4 546	51.9	54.9	69.3
LDCs	301	366	985	32.0	34.6	52.5
LLDCs	142	167	422	30.0	31.3	45.5
SIDS (UN-OHRLLS)	38	42	57	59.5	60.9	67.7
HIPCs (IMF)	228	280	793	34.5	36.8	53.5
BRICS	1 529	1 700	2 374	49.0	52.5	68.2
G20	2 744	2 974	3 901	58.0	60.8	73.9

Table 4.1.3 | Most populated economies

Economy	Total			Urban		
	Population	Annual growth rate[a]		Share in total population	Annual growth rate[a]	
	(Millions)	(Percentage)		(Percentage)	(Percentage)	
	2020	2015–2020	2020–2050	2020	2015–2020	2020–2050
China	1 439	0.5	-0.1	61.4	2.5	0.8
India	1 380	1.0	0.6	34.9	2.3	2.0
United States of America	334	0.6	0.4	82.8	0.8	0.7
Indonesia	274	1.1	0.6	56.6	2.3	1.5
Pakistan	221	2.0	1.4	37.2	2.7	2.6
Brazil	213	0.8	0.2	87.1	1.1	0.4
Nigeria	206	2.6	2.2	52.0	4.2	3.2
Bangladesh	165	1.1	0.5	38.2	3.2	1.9
Russian Federation	146	0.1	-0.2	74.8	0.3	0.1
Mexico	129	1.1	0.6	80.7	1.5	0.9
Japan	126	-0.2	-0.6	91.8	-0.1	-0.5
Ethiopia	115	2.6	1.9	21.7	4.8	3.9
Philippines	110	1.4	0.9	47.4	1.9	1.8
Egypt	102	2.0	1.5	42.8	2.0	2.4
Viet Nam	97	1.0	0.4	37.3	3.0	1.8
Congo, Dem. Rep. of the	90	3.2	2.6	45.6	4.5	3.7
Turkey	84	1.4	0.5	76.1	2.1	0.9
Iran (Islamic Republic of)	84	1.4	0.7	75.9	2.0	1.1
Germany	84	0.5	-0.1	77.5	0.5	0.1
Thailand	70	0.3	-0.2	51.4	1.8	0.8

[a] Exponential growth rate (see annex 6.3).

4.2 Age structure

Map 4.2 | **Dependency ratio, 2020**
(Percentage)

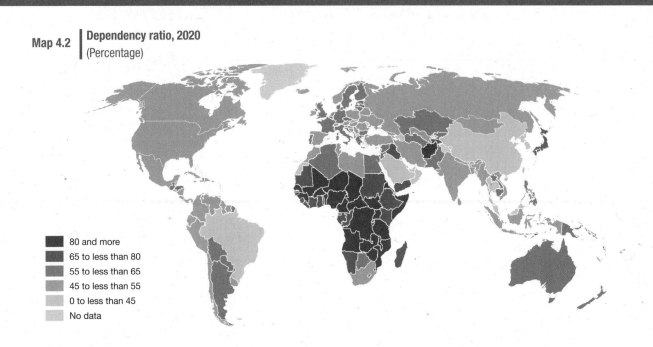

- 80 and more
- 65 to less than 80
- 55 to less than 65
- 45 to less than 55
- 0 to less than 45
- No data

Concepts and definitions

In this section, the term "persons of working age" refers to persons aged from 15 to 64 years. The term "children" refers to persons under the age of 15. The term "older persons" refers to persons over the age of 64.

The dependency ratio is defined as the number of children and older persons per hundred persons of working age. It can be expressed as the sum of the child dependency ratio and the old-age dependency ratio.

The child dependency ratio is defined as the number of children per hundred persons of working age. The old-age dependency ratio is defined as the number of older persons per hundred persons of working age.

Except for the world total, data in this chapter exclude data by sex and age for economies with a population of less than 90 000 in 2019.

Regional distribution of dependency ratios and trends over time

Globally, in 2020, for every 100 persons of working age there were 53 persons who were younger or older. This figure, the dependency ratio, varies considerably across regions. In most economies of Western, Middle and Eastern Africa it is higher than 65 per cent, whereas in Western, Eastern and South-Eastern Asia, it is often lower than 45 per cent. Notable exceptions include Japan (69 per cent) and Israel (67 per cent), as well as Yemen (72 per cent), Timor-Leste (70 per cent) and Iraq (70 per cent).

Globally, for every 100 persons of working age there were 39 children and 14 older people. The proportion of children in the population has steadily declined from the peak of 38 per cent in 1966, to 25 per cent in 2020, while the proportion of the older than 64 rose from 5 to 9 per cent over the same period. The net effect has been a decline of the dependency ratio from 76 to 53 per cent. The aging of the world population is projected to continue in the coming decades.

Figure 4.2.1 | **World population by age group**
(Percentage)

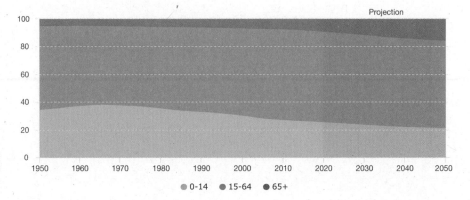

Non-pyramid shape of developed economies' population pyramid

Comparing population pyramids, we find that in developing economies, older age classes are successively smaller than younger classes. In developed economies, this pattern is reversed, so that the proportions of older age groups are larger and younger age groups are smaller than in developing economies.

In both the developing and developed world, women are the majority for older age groups, whereas the majority of children are boys. In 2020, 49.6 per cent of the world population was female.

Figure 4.2.2 | **Population pyramids, 2020**

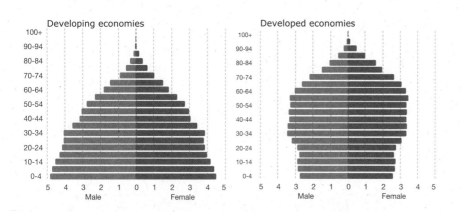

Less child dependency, more old-age dependency

Over the next 30 years, the total dependency ratio is projected to rise in most regions. Child dependency ratios will decrease, but it is forecast that this will be compensated for by rising old-age dependency ratios. Africa is the exception, featuring both decreasing child and overall dependency ratios (child: from 72 per cent in 2020 to 52 per cent in 2050, overall: from 78 to 61 per cent). In general, child dependency ratios are projected to fall fastest where they are currently highest.

Contrary to child dependency, old-age dependency is forecast to increase most in the groups of economies where it is already comparatively high. This is the case in developed economies, where an increase from 30 per cent in 2020 to 46 per cent is expected by 2050.

Figure 4.2.3 | **Dependency ratio by age structure** (Percentage)

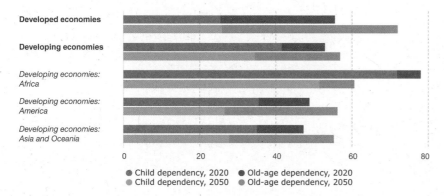

● Child dependency, 2020   ● Old-age dependency, 2020
● Child dependency, 2050   ● Old-age dependency, 2050

Note: The total dependency ratio is the sum of the child and old-age dependency ratios.

Dependency ratio above 65% in many African economies

Globally, the proportion of children fell

from 30% in 2000

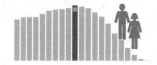 to 25% in 2020

The proportion of people under 30 is smaller in developed than in developing economies

Old-age dependency in **developed** economies is **forecast** to increase

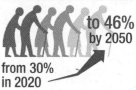 to 46% by 2050

from 30% in 2020

Table 4.2.1 | **Age structure and dependency ratio**

Group of economies	Year	Population (Millions)			Dependency ratio (Percentage)		
		0-14	15-64	65+	Child (0-14)	Old-age (65+)	Total
World	**1950**	**870**	**1 538**	**129**	**56.5**	**8.4**	**64.9**
	2020	**1 984**	**5 084**	**728**	**39.0**	**14.3**	**53.3**
	2050	**2 056**	**6 131**	**1 549**	**33.5**	**25.3**	**58.8**
Developed economies	1950	233	547	65	42.6	11.8	54.5
	2020	212	828	248	25.6	29.9	55.5
	2050	196	755	349	25.9	46.2	72.1
Developing economies	1950	636	991	64	64.2	6.5	70.7
	2020	1 771	4 255	480	41.6	11.3	52.9
	2050	1 860	5 375	1 200	34.6	22.3	56.9
Developing economies: Africa	1950	94	126	7	74.6	5.9	80.5
	2020	541	752	47	71.9	6.2	78.1
	2050	797	1 548	143	51.5	9.2	60.7
Developing economies: America	1950	67	93	6	72.2	6.2	78.4
	2020	155	436	58	35.6	13.3	48.9
	2050	130	485	143	26.7	29.6	56.3
Developing economies: Asia and Oceania	1950	475	772	51	61.5	6.6	68.1
	2020	1 075	3 066	375	35.1	12.2	47.3
	2050	933	3 342	914	27.9	27.3	55.2
Selected groups							
Developing economies excluding China	1950	448	650	39	68.9	6.1	74.9
	2020	1 517	3 242	307	46.8	9.5	56.3
	2050	1 661	4 537	834	36.6	18.4	55.0
Developing economies excluding LDCs	1950	556	883	58	62.9	6.5	69.5
	2020	1 361	3 646	442	37.3	12.1	49.5
	2050	1 289	4 189	1 080	30.8	25.8	56.6
LDCs	1950	80	108	6	74.4	5.9	80.3
	2020	410	609	38	67.4	6.2	73.6
	2050	571	1 186	120	48.1	10.1	58.2
LLDCs	1950	32	42	2	76.2	5.4	81.5
	2020	208	305	20	67.9	6.6	74.6
	2050	274	593	60	46.2	10.1	56.3
SIDS (UN-OHRLLS)	1950	8	12	1	68.9	6.7	75.7
	2020	18	44	6	39.8	12.7	52.4
	2050	17	53	13	32.5	24.2	56.7
HIPCs (IMF)	1950	52	67	4	77.3	5.9	83.2
	2020	322	416	23	77.4	5.5	82.9
	2050	484	925	73	52.3	7.9	60.2
BRICS	1950	411	719	49	57.1	6.9	64.0
	2020	704	2 224	309	31.6	13.9	45.6
	2050	574	2 226	682	25.8	30.6	56.4
G20	1950	645	1 221	107	52.8	8.7	61.6
	2020	1 022	3 306	566	30.9	17.1	48.0
	2050	862	3 305	1 110	26.1	33.6	59.7

Table 4.2.2 | Population by age class, 2020

Group of economies	Population (Millions)	Percentage of total						
		All age classes	0-14	15-24	25-39	40-64	65-74	75+
World	**7 795**	**100.0**	**25.4**	**15.5**	**22.4**	**27.3**	**5.9**	**3.5**
Developed economies	1 288	100.0	16.5	11.0	19.9	33.3	10.5	8.7
Developing economies	6 506	100.0	27.2	16.4	22.9	26.1	5.0	2.4
Developing economies: Africa	1 339	100.0	40.4	19.3	20.5	16.4	2.5	1.0
Developing economies: America	650	100.0	23.9	16.5	23.4	27.3	5.5	3.4
Developing economies: Asia and Oceania	4 517	100.0	23.8	15.5	23.5	28.8	5.6	2.7
Selected groups								
Developing economies excluding China	5 067	100.0	29.9	17.7	22.9	23.4	4.0	2.1
LDCs	1 057	100.0	38.8	20.0	20.8	16.8	2.4	1.1
LLDCs	533	100.0	38.9	19.7	20.9	16.7	2.6	1.2
SIDS (UN-OHRLLS)	68	100.0	26.1	16.4	22.8	26.4	5.2	3.1
Selected economies								
China	1 439	100.0	17.7	11.8	22.7	35.8	8.3	3.7
India	1 380	100.0	26.2	18.0	24.1	25.1	4.5	2.1
Brazil	213	100.0	20.7	15.7	24.2	29.8	6.0	3.6
Nigeria	206	100.0	43.5	19.4	19.2	15.2	2.1	0.6
Russian Federation	146	100.0	18.4	9.4	22.9	33.8	9.5	6.0
Japan	126	100.0	12.4	9.3	16.3	33.6	13.8	14.6

Table 4.2.3 | Female population by age class, 2020

Group of economies	Population (Millions)	Percentage female						
		All age classes	0-14	15-24	25-39	40-64	65-74	75+
World	**3 865**	**49.6**	**48.4**	**48.3**	**48.9**	**50.1**	**52.8**	**58.9**
Developed economies	660	51.3	48.7	48.8	49.3	51.0	54.4	61.1
Developing economies	3 204	49.2	48.3	48.3	48.8	49.9	52.2	57.3
Developing economies: Africa	670	50.0	49.3	49.6	50.1	51.2	54.0	58.3
Developing economies: America	330	50.8	49.0	49.4	50.3	52.0	54.3	59.0
Developing economies: Asia and Oceania	2 204	48.8	47.8	47.6	48.3	49.4	51.7	56.9
Selected groups								
Developing economies excluding China	2 503	49.4	48.6	48.6	49.0	50.1	52.7	57.4
LDCs	531	50.3	49.4	49.7	50.7	51.5	53.9	56.8
LLDCs	269	50.4	49.2	49.6	50.9	52.0	55.5	59.8
SIDS (UN-OHRLLS)	33	49.4	48.9	48.8	48.2	50.0	52.4	56.6
Selected economies								
China	701	48.7	46.6	46.7	48.2	49.3	51.3	57.1
India	663	48.0	47.5	47.1	47.5	48.8	50.6	54.1
Brazil	108	50.9	48.9	49.2	50.0	51.8	54.9	60.4
Nigeria	102	49.3	48.9	49.2	49.3	50.2	52.6	53.3
Russian Federation	78	53.7	48.7	48.9	49.8	54.2	62.5	73.8
Japan	65	51.2	48.7	48.7	48.8	49.5	52.0	60.6

5

Maritime transport

KEY FIGURES **2020**

Seaborne trade volume

10.6 billion tons

Change of seaborne trade

-3.8%

World commercial fleet capacity
(as of 31 December)

2.1 billion dwt

Global container port traffic

816 million TEUs

5.1 World seaborne trade

Map 5.1 | **Tonnage loaded and discharged, 2020**
(Billions of tons)

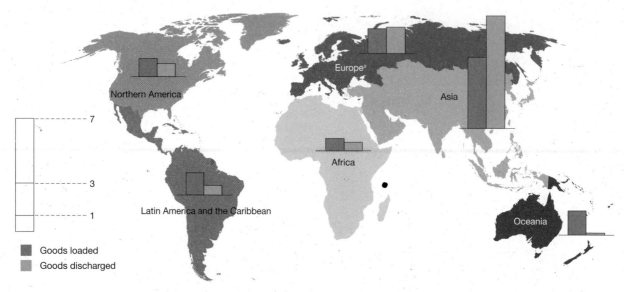

Goods loaded
Goods discharged

a Including the Russian Federation and the French overseas departments.

Concepts and definitions

The figures on seaborne trade in this section measure the volumes of international shipments, in metric tons, of goods loaded and discharged in the world's seaports. Cabotage and transshipments are not included.

Goods loaded for international shipment are assumed to be exports, while goods discharged from ships are assumed to be imports. The seaborne trade balance measures the difference between the volumes of loaded and discharged goods.

Dry cargo refers to cargo that is usually not carried in tankers, such as dry bulks (e.g., coal, ores, grains), pallets, bags, crates, and containers. "Other" tanker trade refers to tanker trade, excluding crude oil. It includes refined petroleum products, gas and chemicals.

The data presented in this section have been compiled from various sources, including country reports as well as port industry and other specialist websites (see UNCTAD 2021d).

Trends and geography of world seaborne trade in 2020

The COVID-19 pandemic weighed on international maritime trade while disrupting operations and causing supply chain pressures. The volume of maritime trade slumped by 3.8 per cent in 2020 to a total of 10.6 billion tons.

The predominance of Asia as a leading maritime freight area continued unabated. In 2020, Asian ports, including developed and developing regions, loaded around 4.4 billion tons of goods, amounting to over 41.3 per cent of total goods loaded in ports worldwide. About 7.0 billion tons equivalent to 65.5 per cent of total goods discharged worldwide, were received by Asian ports in 2020.

Of the total freight shipped internationally in 2020, 7.7 billion tons, or 72 per cent, was dry cargo. Over time, dry cargo has expanded its share, now accounting for nearly three quarters of total maritime trade volumes. A decade ago, this share was closer to two thirds.

Figure 5.1.1 | **Goods loaded worldwide**
(Billions of tons)

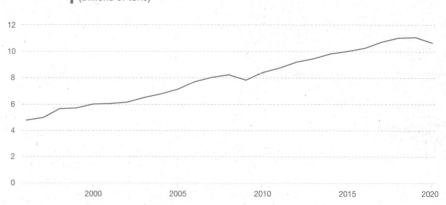

Contribution of developing economies

In 2020, developing economies still accounted for the largest share of global seaborne trade, both in terms of exports and imports. They loaded 59.5 per cent and discharged 69.5 per cent of the world total. Asian and Oceanian developing economies contributed most to those shares. While developing economies remain the main maritime trade centres, the structure of their trade has changed over the years with their share of world seaborne imports increasingly surpassing their share of exports since 2013.

Figure 5.1.2 | **Seaborne trade of developing economies**
(Percentage of corresponding world tonnage)

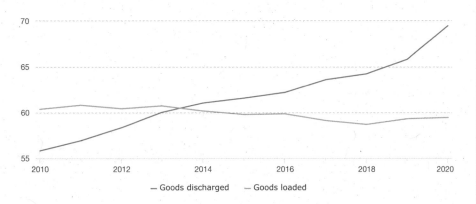

— Goods discharged   — Goods loaded

Developments in seaborne trade balances

The structural shift in the composition of economies' maritime trade and total imports and exports is reflected in the widening maritime trade deficit for developing economies and surplus for developed economies. Developing economies loaded 401 million tons more goods in 2010 than they discharged. This compared to a deficit of 149 million tons in 2015, which deepened to 1 055 million tons in 2020. This development was mainly driven by a widening deficit in Asian developing economies. Much of the deficit increase in 2020 reflects the active role of Eastern Asia and especially continued import demand in China. On the other hand, the surplus for developed economies increased in 2020, expressing a decline in import demand largely induced by the COVID-19 pandemic, among other issues.[1]

[1] For further analyses on this topic, see UNCTAD (2021d).

Figure 5.1.3 | **Seaborne trade balance**
(Millions of tons)

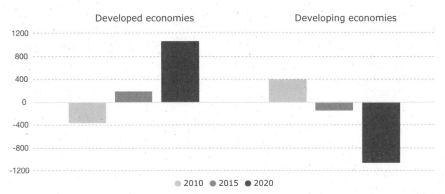

● 2010 ● 2015 ● 2020

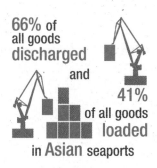

Seaborne trade growth **slumped**

-3.8% in 2020

66% of all goods **discharged** and **41%** of all goods **loaded** in **Asian** seaports

Developing economies' **share** of **seaborne** trade **imports** rose to **69.5% in 2020**

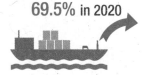

Developed economies' **seaborne** trade **balance reached**

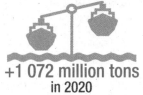

+1 072 million tons in 2020

Table 5.1.1 | Total seaborne trade by group of economies

| Group of economies | Loaded | | | Discharged | | | Balance | |
	Volume (Millions of tons)		Annual growth rate (Percentage)	Volume (Millions of tons)		Annual growth rate (Percentage)	Volume (Millions of tons)	
	2015	2020	2020	2015	2020	2020	2015	2020
World[a]	**10 013**	**10 648**	**-3.8**	**9 965**	**10 631**	**-3.8**	**48**	**17**
Developed economies	4 026	4 317	-4.1	3 829	3 245	-14.1	197	1 072
Developing economies	5 987	6 331	-3.6	6 136	7 386	1.5	-149	-1 055
Developing economies: Africa	715	735	-9.7	475	510	-4.4	240	225
Developing economies: America	1 352	1 369	-2.7	590	590	-5.0	762	779
Developing economies: Asia and Oceania	3 921	4 226	-2.8	5 071	6 286	2.7	-1 151	-2 059

[a] Annual world totals of goods loaded and discharged are not necessarily the same, given bilateral asymmetries in international merchandise trade statistics and that goods loaded in one calendar year may reach their port of destination in the next calendar year.

Table 5.1.2 | Seaborne trade by cargo type and group of economies

Crude oil

| Group of economies | Loaded | | | Discharged | | | Balance | |
	Volume (Millions of tons)		Annual growth rate (Percentage)	Volume (Millions of tons)		Annual growth rate (Percentage)	Volume (Millions of tons)	
	2015	2020	2020	2015	2020	2020	2015	2020
World[a]	**1 761**	**1 716**	**-7.8**	**1 910**	**1 864**	**-7.9**	**-149**	**-148**
Developed economies	294	426	-6.1	995	732	-18.8	-701	-307
Developing economies	1 467	1 290	-8.3	915	1 131	0.9	551	159
Developing economies: Africa	294	236	-22.0	39	31	-13.4	254	206
Developing economies: America	223	200	-9.7	66	40	-12.0	158	161
Developing economies: Asia and Oceania	950	854	-3.2	810	1 061	2.0	139	-207

[a] Annual world totals of goods loaded and discharged are not necessarily the same, given bilateral asymmetries in international merchandise trade statistics and that goods loaded in one calendar year may reach their port of destination in the next calendar year.

Other tanker trade

| Group of economies | Loaded | | | Discharged | | | Balance | |
	Volume (Millions of tons)		Annual growth rate (Percentage)	Volume (Millions of tons)		Annual growth rate (Percentage)	Volume (Millions of tons)	
	2015	2020	2020	2015	2020	2020	2015	2020
World[a]	**1 178**	**1 202**	**-7.7**	**1 175**	**1 222**	**-7.5**	**3**	**-20**
Developed economies	510	430	-9.8	535	370	-20.1	-24	60
Developing economies	668	772	-6.5	641	852	-0.6	27	-80
Developing economies: Africa	59	83	-9.0	72	108	-4.8	-14	-25
Developing economies: America	84	76	-7.0	102	130	-9.6	-18	-54
Developing economies: Asia and Oceania	525	613	-6.1	467	614	2.3	59	-1

[a] Annual world totals of goods loaded and discharged are not necessarily the same, given bilateral asymmetries in international merchandise trade statistics and that goods loaded in one calendar year may reach their port of destination in the next calendar year.

Dry cargo

Group of economies	Loaded			Discharged			Balance	
	Volume		Annual growth rate	Volume		Annual growth rate	Volume	
	(Millions of tons)		(Percentage)	(Millions of tons)		(Percentage)	(Millions of tons)	
	2015	2020	2020	2015	2020	2020	2015	2020
World[a]	**7 074**	**7 730**	**-2.2**	**6 879**	**7 545**	**-2.2**	**195**	**185**
Developed economies	3 222	3 461	-3.1	2 300	2 142	-11.2	922	1 319
Developing economies	3 853	4 269	-1.5	4 579	5 403	2.0	-727	-1 134
Developing economies: Africa	363	416	-0.9	364	372	-3.5	-1	44
Developing economies: America	1 044	1 093	-0.9	422	420	-2.8	623	673
Developing economies: Asia and Oceania	2 446	2 760	-1.9	3 794	4 611	2.9	-1 348	-1 851

[a] Annual world totals of goods loaded and discharged are not necessarily the same, given bilateral asymmetries in international merchandise trade statistics and that goods loaded in one calendar year may reach their port of destination in the next calendar year.

Table 5.1.3 | **Development of goods loaded worldwide by type of cargo**
(Millions of tons)

Year	Total goods	Crude oil	Other tanker trade	Dry cargo
1975	3 072	1 364	280	1 428
1980	3 704	1 527	344	1 833
1985	3 330	1 049	410	1 895
1990	4 008	1 287	468	2 253
1995	4 651	1 532	518	2 601
2000	5 984	1 605	558	3 821
2005	7 109	1 857	565	4 687
2010	8 401	1 785	968	5 649
2015	10 013	1 761	1 178	7 074
2020	10 648	1 716	1 202	7 730

5.2 Merchant fleet

Map 5.2 | **Building, ownership, registration and recycling of ships, 2020**
(Percentage of world total)

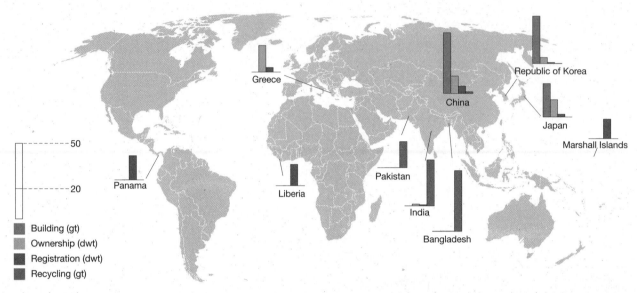

Sources: UNCTADstat (UNCTAD, 2021), Clarksons Research.
Note: Top three countries in each segment are shown. Building and recycling are estimated deliveries and demolitions during 2020. Registration and ownership figures refer to the beginning of the year 2021.

Concepts and definitions

The unit dead-weight tons (dwt) is used to indicate the cargo carrying capacity of a ship, while gross tons (gt) reflect its size. The latter is relevant to measure shipbuilding and recycling activity, while the former is used to capture the capacity to transport cargo.

The presented statistics on fleet registration (the flag of a ship), shipbuilding and recycling cover all commercial ships of 100 gt and more. The market shares for ownership only cover larger ships of 1000 gt and above, as the true ownership is not always known for smaller vessels.

World fleet development and composition

In January 2021, the world fleet reached a carrying capacity of 2.1 billion dwt, 63 million dwt more than the previous year. Over recent years, tonnage has increased considerably in all segments except general cargo carriers. Bulk carriers recorded an especially rapid increase. Between 2011 and 2021, their share in total carrying capacity rose from 39 to 43 per cent, whereas the share of oil tankers shrank from 31 to 29 per cent, and the share of general cargo from 6 to 4 per cent.

Shipbuilding and recycling

In 2020, global shipbuilding was concentrated in China, the Republic of Korea and Japan. These three economies accounted for 94 per cent of shipbuilding in terms of gross tonnage. In ship recycling, Bangladesh and India jointly accounted for 71 per cent and Pakistan for an additional 17 per cent.

Figure 5.2.1 | **World fleet by principal vessel type**
(Millions of dead-weight tons)

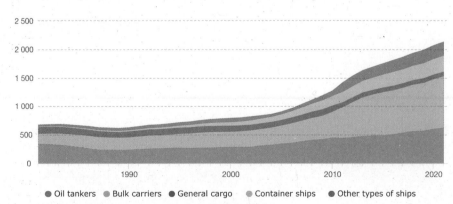

Sources: UNCTADstat (UNCTAD, 2021a); Clarksons Research.
Note: Commercial ships of 100 gt and above. Beginning-of-year figures.

Fleet ownership

As of January 2021, the top five ship-owning economies combined accounted for 52 per cent of world fleet tonnage. Greece held a market share of 18 per cent, followed by China (12 per cent), Japan (11 per cent), Singapore (7 per cent), and Hong Kong SAR (5 per cent). Half of the world's tonnage was owned by Asian companies. Owners from Europe accounted for 40 per cent and owners from Northern America for 6 per cent. Companies from Africa and from Latin America and the Caribbean had a share of just over one per cent; Oceania just below one.

Figure 5.2.2 | **Fleet market by region of beneficial ownership, 2021**
(Millions of dead-weight tons)

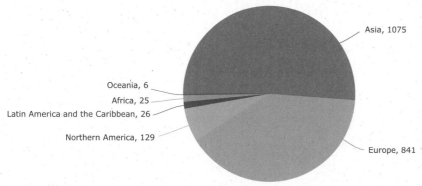

Sources: UNCTADstat (UNCTAD, 2021a); Clarksons Research.
Note: Commercial ships of 1000 gt and above. Beginning-of-year figures.

Major flags of registration

Many commercial ships are registered under a flag that does not match the nationality of the vessel owner. For example, at the beginning of 2021, more than half of all ships owned by Japanese entities were registered in Panama; of the ships owned by Greek entities, 25 per cent were registered in Liberia and another 22 per cent in the Marshall Islands.

Panama (344 million dwt), Liberia (300 million dwt) and the Marshall Islands (274 million dwt) represented the leading flags of registration. Hong Kong SAR and Singapore followed in fourth and fifth place, respectively. Among these five, the Marshall Islands recorded the strongest increase in registrations over the last decade.

Figure 5.2.3 | **Vessels capacity in top 5 registries**
(Millions of dead-weight tons)

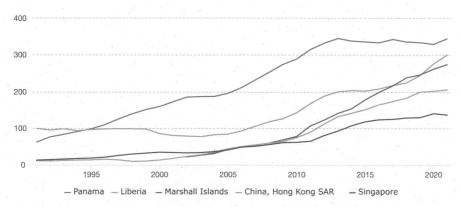

— Panama — Liberia — Marshall Islands — China, Hong Kong SAR — Singapore

Sources: UNCTADstat (UNCTAD, 2021a); Clarksons Research.
Note: Commercial ships of 100 gt and above. Beginning-of-year figures. Ranked by the values as of 1 January 2021.

World commercial fleet grew by 63 million dwt

between January 2020 and January 2021

94% of global shipbuilding occurred in China, the Republic of Korea and Japan in 2020

Half of the world fleet owned by Asian companies

16% of the global fleet carrying capacity

registered in Panama

Table 5.2.1 | Merchant fleet registration by group of economies

Group of economies	2016				2021			
	Tonnage		Vessels		Tonnage		Vessels	
	(Millions of dwt)	Share in world (Percentage)	(Thousands)	Share in world (Percentage)	(Millions of dwt)	Share in world (Percentage)	(Thousands)	Share in world (Percentage)
World	**1 811**	**100.0**	**92**	**100.0**	**2 135**	**100.0**	**100**	**100.0**
Developed economies	423	23.3	29	31.4	454	21.3	29	29.2
Developing economies	1 384	76.4	61	66.5	1 676	78.5	69	69.2
Developing economies: Africa	237	13.1	6	6.9	326	15.3	8	7.9
Developing economies: America	452	25.0	16	17.6	458	21.5	16	16.1
Developing economies: Asia and Oceania	695	38.4	39	42.0	892	41.8	45	45.2
Selected groups								
Developing economies excluding China	1 307	72.2	57	61.9	1 568	73.5	62	62.5
Developing economies excluding LDCs	1 151	63.6	55	59.8	1 358	63.6	62	62.2
LDCs	233	12.9	6	6.6	318	14.9	7	7.0
LLDCs	5	0.3	1	1.2	3	0.1	1	1.1
SIDS (UN-OHRLLS)	451	24.9	14	15.0	533	25.0	14	14.2
HIPCs (IMF)	227	12.5	5	5.8	313	14.7	6	6.5
BRICS	107	5.9	9	10.0	141	6.6	12	12.3
G20	535	29.5	45	48.9	615	28.8	50	50.5

Sources: UNCTADstat (UNCTAD, 2021a); Clarksons Research.
Note: Commercial ships of 100 gt and above. Figures refer to the beginning of the year.

Table 5.2.2 | **Fleet ownership and registration, main economies, 1 January 2021**

Vessels
(Number of vessels)

Economy of ownership (Ranked by number of ships owned)	Flag of registration (Ranked by number of ships registered)							
	Panama	China	Liberia	Marshall Islands	Singapore	China, Hong Kong SAR	Indonesia	World
China	655	4 887	152	103	62	935	8	7 318
Greece	465	0	1 101	1 055	28	20	2	4 705
Japan	2 066	0	252	234	169	54	7	4 029
Singapore	282	4	242	137	1 459	134	95	2 843
Germany	34	0	580	96	74	18	0	2 395
Indonesia	16	2	7	9	8	1	2 232	2 321
Norway	48	0	89	132	81	50	4	2 042
United States of America	67	0	95	318	8	37	1	1 813
Russian Federation	34	0	117	0	2	1	0	1 786
China, Hong Kong SAR	324	20	53	69	51	886	3	1 764
World	**6 653**	**4 933**	**3 909**	**3 732**	**2 541**	**2 440**	**2 398**	**53 973**

Sources: UNCTADstat (UNCTAD, 2021a); Clarksons Research.
Note: Commercial ships of 1000 gt and above.

Tonnage
(Thousands of dead-weight tons)

Economy of ownership (Ranked by tonnage owned)	Flag of registration (Ranked by tonnage registered)							
	Panama	Liberia	Marshall Islands	China, Hong Kong SAR	Singapore	Malta	China	World
Greece	27 924	94 234	80 325	1 262	1 763	63 639	0	373 417
China	23 461	11 564	6 505	81 330	4 964	2 951	105 657	244 556
Japan	136 971	24 099	14 510	3 143	10 130	829	0	241 848
Singapore	11 884	18 655	8 972	7 248	73 258	3 198	964	139 064
China, Hong Kong SAR	12 600	5 785	3 528	72 367	4 878	839	135	104 219
Germany	870	33 112	5 019	1 296	3 844	5 795	0	86 197
Korea, Republic of	40 042	1 379	26 474	1 089	29	356	2	86 093
Norway	1 993	5 027	8 384	8 742	4 622	1 339	0	64 043
Bermuda	1 495	7 500	21 472	8 169	1 247	172	0	64 034
France	4 400	11 132	17 686	2 700	1 261	7 379	0	57 023
World	**343 601**	**300 076**	**274 016**	**205 011**	**136 164**	**116 373**	**106 879**	**2 116 401**

Sources: UNCTADstat (UNCTAD, 2021a); Clarksons Research.
Note: Commercial ships of 1000 gt and above.

5.3 Maritime transport indicators

Map 5.3 | **Liner shipping connectivity, 2021**

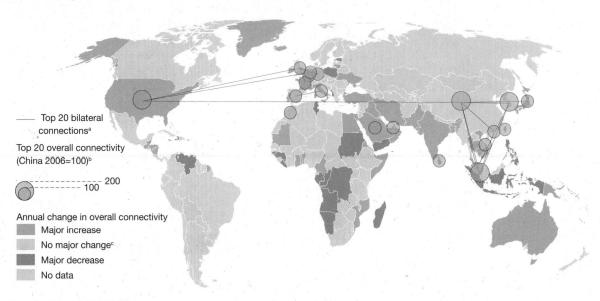

a As indicated by the LSBCI 2021.
b As indicated by the LSCI.
c Change of less than 5 per cent compared to the value in the previous year.

Concepts and definitions

The liner shipping connectivity index (LSCI) indicates a country's position within global liner shipping networks. It is calculated from the number of ship calls, their container carrying capacity, the number of services and companies, the size of the largest ship, and the number of other countries connected through direct liner shipping services.

The liner shipping bilateral connectivity index (LSBCI) is calculated from five components, including the number of transshipments required to trade and the connections available using one transshipment.

Port container traffic is measured in twenty-foot equivalent units (TEUs). One TEU represents the volume of a standard 20-feet long intermodal container.

The number of port calls and the time spent in ports are derived from combining automatic identification system data with port mapping intelligence. These data cover ships of 1000 gt and above.

Liner shipping connectivity throughout the world

In the third quarter of 2021, China was the economy best connected to the global liner shipping network, as measured by the LSCI. Singapore, the Republic of Korea, Malaysia and the United States of America followed next in the rankings. Regional leaders included: the Netherlands and Spain in Europe; Panama and Colombia in Latin America and the Caribbean; Egypt and Morocco in Africa; and Sri Lanka and India in Southern Asia. Among the least connected 30 economies, 22 are islands and four are coastal LDCs.

In 2021, nine of the top 10 bilateral connections were intra-regional within Europe or within Eastern and South-Eastern Asia. The only inter-regional connection among the top 20 was between China and the United States of America.

Figure 5.3.1 | **Liner shipping connectivity index, top 5 economies** (China Q1 2006 = 100)

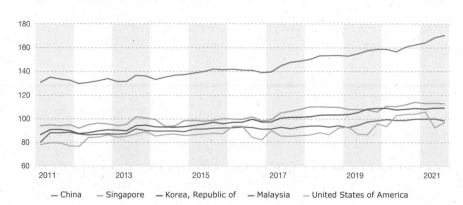

Port container traffic

In 2020, 815.6 million TEUs of containers were handled in ports worldwide. World container port throughput declined by 1.2 per cent between 2019 and 2020. This reduction is moderate in comparison to other shipping market segments and total seaborne trade (see section 5.1). This reflects the resilience of containerized trade amid the disruption caused by the COVID-19 pandemic.

Figure 5.3.2 | **World container port throughput**
(Millions of twenty-foot equivalent units)

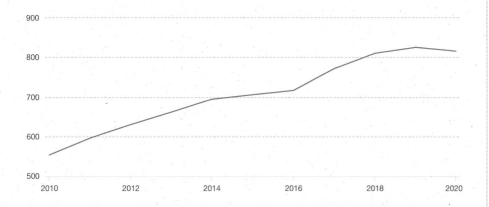

Asia's leading role as a global maritime freight loading and unloading centre (see section 5.1) and its high liner shipping connectivity are mirrored in the region's high contribution to containerized port throughput. In 2020, ports in the developing economies of Asia and Oceania handled 509 million TEUs of containers, accounting for 62 per cent of world port container traffic. The shares of developing America and developing Africa were significantly lower, at 7 and 4 per cent, respectively. Developed economies accounted for 26 per cent.

Port calls

The economy that recorded most port calls of ships in 2020 was Norway. On average, cargo-carrying ships departed from Norwegian ports less than half a day after their arrival.[1]

[1] For further analyses on that topic, see UNCTAD (2021d).

Figure 5.3.3 | **Containerized port traffic by group of economies, 2020**
(Millions of twenty-foot equivalent units)

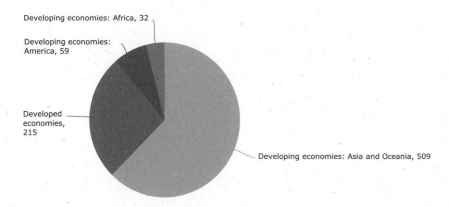

China, Singapore and the Republic of Korea are most integrated into global liner shipping networks

Bilateral connectivity is highest within continents, rather than between

World container port throughput declined: -1.2 % in 2020

Developing economies in Asia and Oceania handled 62% of world port container traffic in 2020

Table 5.3.1 | **Liner shipping connectivity index of most connected economies, by region**
(China Q1 2006 = 100)

	Economy (Ranked by Q3 2021 value)	Q1 2010	Q1 2015	Q1 2020	Q1 2021	Q2 2021	Q3 2021
Northern America and Europe	1. United States of America	75	86	93	106	106	97
	2. Netherlands	80	81	92	92	92	91
	3. Spain	74	80	89	90	90	91
	4. United Kingdom	80	85	90	91	91	89
	5. Belgium	80	84	89	88	88	88
Latin America and the Caribbean	1. Panama	33	42	49	50	50	51
	2. Colombia	29	41	48	49	49	50
	3. Mexico	33	41	49	49	49	48
	4. Dominican Republic	25	26	38	38	38	43
	5. Peru	23	31	40	39	39	41
Africa	1. Morocco	45	58	69	69	69	70
	2. Egypt	45	57	61	68	68	67
	3. South Africa	32	38	40	41	41	39
	4. Ghana	20	22	37	40	40	37
	5. Togo	15	26	35	37	37	36
Asia	1. China	118	139	159	164	164	170
	2. Singapore	90	98	110	113	113	113
	3. Korea, Republic of	73	94	109	108	108	109
	4. Malaysia	72	91	99	100	100	98
	5. China, Hong Kong SAR	88	92	94	94	94	93
Oceania	1. Australia	29	33	34	38	38	36
	2. New Zealand	19	22	29	29	29	30
	3. French Polynesia	10	9	14	14	14	15
	4. Papua New Guinea	7	10	10	11	11	11
	5. New Caledonia	12	12	10	11	11	11

Table 5.3.2 | **Time at port, by market segment, in the top 20 economies by port call, 2020**

Economy	Number of port calls	Median time at port (days)						
		All market segments	Liquid bulk	Container ship	Dry breakbulk	Dry bulk	LPG carriers	LNG carriers
1 Norway	584 421	0.4	0.6	0.3	0.3	0.8	0.8	0.3
2 China	261 269	1.1	1.1	0.6	1.3	2.0	1.0	1.2
3 Japan	259 583	0.4	0.3	0.3	1.1	0.8	0.3	1.0
4 United States of America[a]	246 863	1.5	1.6	1.0	1.9	2.0	2.0	1.3
5 Italy	200 074	1.3	1.3	0.9	2.0	3.5	1.6	..
6 Turkey	169 964	1.2	1.2	0.6	1.5	3.9	1.3	1.3
7 Indonesia	166 578	1.2	1.2	1.0	1.1	3.1	1.1	1.4
8 United Kingdom[b]	158 231	1.1	1.0	0.7	1.5	2.7	1.1	1.3
9 Greece	136 718	0.8	0.6	1.0	1.2	0.4	1.0	1.2
10 Netherlands	117 420	0.6	0.5	0.8	0.4	0.8	1.0	1.0
11 Spain	105 046	0.9	0.9	0.7	1.2	1.8	1.0	1.0
12 Canada	103 297	0.8	1.1	1.8	0.6	0.4	1.5	..
13 Denmark	102 178	0.8	0.7	0.4	0.9	0.9	1.0	..
14 Germany	88 445	0.8	0.5	1.0	1.0	2.4	0.8	..
15 Korea, Republic of	73 563	0.9	0.8	0.6	1.2	2.0	0.9	1.0
16 Sweden	67 477	0.8	0.7	0.6	1.1	0.5	0.8	0.8
17 Russian Federation	67 438	1.4	1.1	1.3	1.6	2.4	1.4	1.1
18 Croatia	60 198	1.1	0.9	0.6	2.3	2.4	..	..
19 France[c]	58 537	1.1	1.1	0.8	1.6	2.9	1.1	1.2
20 Australia	58 474	1.5	1.3	1.4	2.0	1.6	0.9	1.2

Note: Number of port calls includes arrivals of ferries, roll-on roll-off and passenger ships, for which the time in port is not computed.
[a] Excluding Puerto Rico and United States Virgin Islands.
[b] United Kingdom of Great Britain and Northern Ireland excluding Channel Islands and Isle of Man.
[c] Excluding French Guiana, Guadeloupe, Martinique, Mayotte, Monaco and Reunion.

Table 5.3.3 | **Liner shipping connectivity of the world's seven most connected economies**

Economy (Ranked by LSCI 2021)	Year	LSCI (China Q1 2006=100)	LSBCI vis-à-vis ...						
			China	Singapore	Korea, Rep. of	United States of America	Malaysia	China, Hong Kong SAR	Netherlands
China	2016	142	–	0.554	0.622	0.552	0.562	0.563	0.469
	2021	164	–	0.568	0.634	0.556	0.578	0.551	0.474
Singapore	2016	100		–	0.501	0.420	0.580	0.504	0.443
	2021	113		–	0.521	0.443	0.588	0.502	0.467
Korea, Republic of	2016	97			–	0.432	0.504	0.517	0.441
	2021	108			–	0.461	0.505	0.462	0.460
United States of America	2016	93				–	0.393	0.447	0.442
	2021	106				–	0.463	0.456	0.506
Malaysia	2016	92					–	0.507	0.429
	2021	100					–	0.488	0.439
China, Hong Kong SAR	2016	90						–	0.429
	2021	94						–	0.445
Netherlands	2016	83							–
	2021	92							–

Note: All index values refer to the value at Q1 of the indicated year.

6

Annexes

6.1 Key indicators by economy, 2020

Economy	Merchandise trade			Trade in services		GDP	
	Exports	Imports	Terms of trade	Exports	Imports	Per capita (nominal)	Growth (real)[a]
	(Millions of US$)	(Millions of US$)	(2015=100)	(Millions of US$)	(Millions of US$)	(US$)	(Percentage)
World	**17 619 005**	**17 827 911**	**100**	**4 984 187**	**4 680 843**	**10 892**	**-3.6**
Developed economies	9 527 466	10 318 539	101	3 577 949	3 038 501	39 185	-4.8
Albania	2 506	5 570	104	2 558	1 343	5 090	-6.5
Andorra	(e) 117	(e) 1 446	..	..	..	(u) 40 930	-2.0
Australia	250 578	211 109	131	(e) 48 532	(e) 38 479	52 742	-2.4
Austria	168 538	172 200	98	64 882	55 900	47 573	-6.7
Belarus	29 034	32 601	98	8 785	4 935	6 245	-0.9
Belgium	419 892	396 132	101	116 113	115 300	44 375	-6.3
Bermuda	11	785	97	(e) 1 041	(e) 816	108 161	-8.5
Bosnia and Herzegovina	6 152	9 873	103	1 310	517	5 949	-4.5
Bulgaria	31 907	35 038	103	8 121	4 737	9 726	-4.2
Canada	390 599	414 165	97	(e) 85 505	(e) 91 250	43 542	-5.4
Croatia	17 167	26 719	96	9 714	3 974	13 634	-8.4
Cyprus	3 057	8 598	89	12 719	9 428	26 529	-5.0
Czechia	192 057	170 584	102	26 076	21 548	22 536	-5.6
Denmark	108 274	97 561	103	74 801	69 550	61 183	-2.7
Estonia	16 381	17 341	105	6 464	6 224	23 399	-2.9
Faroe Islands	1 284	1 243	101	-	-	..	..
Finland	66 192	68 134	97	28 957	31 768	49 001	-2.8
France	488 372	582 564	98	245 578	231 664	38 565	-8.3
Germany	1 380 647	1 170 441	102	310 661	308 800	45 238	-5.3
Gibraltar	(e) 269	(e) 750	101	-	-	..	..
Greece	35 169	55 691	95	25 940	17 628	18 178	-8.2
Greenland	766	831	104	-	-	56 528	2.0
Holy See	..	..	..	..	..	..	..
Hungary	120 311	115 353	106	22 353	17 843	15 977	-5.1
Iceland	4 586	5 698	91	2 784	2 245	62 003	-6.6
Ireland	179 772	98 750	95	262 704	295 745	84 941	2.5
Israel	49 763	69 985	95	(e) 52 569	(e) 25 332	46 529	-2.5
Italy	496 120	422 875	105	87 346	93 031	31 180	-8.9
Japan	641 319	635 460	106	(e) 160 287	(e) 184 531	39 420	-4.8
Latvia	16 201	18 363	104	5 028	2 957	17 789	-3.6
Lithuania	32 767	33 140	102	12 301	6 585	20 453	-0.9
Luxembourg	13 803	20 929	93	110 783	86 542	117 039	-1.3
Malta	2 680	5 223	111	15 851	13 221	32 231	-7.0
Moldova, Republic of	2 485	5 416	113	1 277	888	2 866	-7.0
Montenegro	419	2 402	..	769	559	7 921	-12.0
Netherlands	674 870	596 012	100	186 644	169 252	53 158	-3.7
New Zealand	38 919	37 152	113	(e) 11 714	(e) 11 226	43 368	-1.3
North Macedonia	6 635	8 710	96	1 646	1 154	5 957	-4.5

| Current account balance | FDI | | CPI growth | Population | | | Fleet size[b] | Economy |
| | Outflows | Inflows | | Total | Share of urban | Old-age dependency ratio | | |
(Millions of US$)	(Millions of US$)	(Millions of US$)	(Percentage)	(Thousands)	(Percentage)	(Percentage)	(1000 of dwt)	
443 078	739 872	998 891	2.8	7 794 799	56.2	14.3	2 134 640	**World**
5 412	353 937	328 540	0.9	1 288 058	79.2	29.9	454 245	Developed economies
-1 318	89	1 107	1.6	2 878	62.1	21.6	49	Albania
..	..	..	-	77	87.9	..	..	Andorra
34 373	9 172	20 146	0.9	25 500	86.2	25.1	2 411	Australia
10 781	-3 213	-17 340	1.4	9 006	58.7	28.9	0	Austria
-241	82	1 397	5.5	9 449	79.5	23.2	1	Belarus
-933	10 227	8 437	0.4	11 590	98.1	30.2	9 603	Belgium
(e) -32	341	114	0.0	62	100.0	..	8 053	Bermuda
-635	-5	371	-0.6	3 281	49.0	26.5	..	Bosnia and Herzegovina
-538	204	2 426	1.2	6 948	75.7	33.6	137	Bulgaria
-29 722	48 655	23 823	0.7	37 742	81.6	27.4	3 361	Canada
-532	235	1 304	0.3	4 105	57.6	33.1	1 800	Croatia
-2 850	-5 954	-3 647	-1.1	891	66.8	20.9	33 976	Cyprus
8 845	3 142	6 293	3.2	10 709	74.1	31.4	..	Czechia
29 319	4 395	1 151	0.3	5 792	88.1	31.7	24 813	Denmark
-244	218	3 156	-0.6	1 327	69.2	32.3	83	Estonia
..	..	..	..	49	42.4	..	410	Faroe Islands
2 052	6 604	2 575	0.4	5 541	85.5	36.6	1 131	Finland
-49 842	44 203	17 932	0.5	67 555	81.3	33.3	7 873	France
266 326	34 950	35 651	0.4	83 784	77.5	33.7	7 618	Germany
..	..	..	..	34	100.0	..	1 951	Gibraltar
-12 699	703	3 572	-1.3	10 423	79.7	34.8	64 850	Greece
..	..	..	2.1	57	87.3	..	1	Greenland
..	..	..	..	1	100.0	..	..	Holy See
20	4 282	4 169	3.3	9 660	71.9	30.8	0	Hungary
198	-276	-811	2.9	341	93.9	24.1	16	Iceland
19 294	-49 474	33 424	-0.5	4 938	63.7	22.6	389	Ireland
20 642	5 860	24 758	-0.6	8 656	92.6	20.8	446	Israel
69 735	10 357	-388	-0.1	60 462	71.0	36.6	11 255	Italy
164 497	115 703	10 254	0.0	126 476	91.8	48.0	39 091	Japan
1 004	268	873	0.1	1 886	68.3	32.9	102	Latvia
4 700	-285	479	1.1	2 722	68.0	32.3	230	Lithuania
2 999	127 087	62 145	0.0	626	91.5	20.5	1 390	Luxembourg
-515	7 288	3 917	0.8	442	94.7	33.2	116 407	Malta
-796	-12	55	3.8	4 034	42.8	17.4	533	Moldova, Republic of
-1 237	-5	529	-0.2	628	67.5	23.8	142	Montenegro
63 655	-161 051	-115 300	1.1	17 135	92.2	31.2	6 807	Netherlands
-1 815	880	4 216	1.7	4 822	86.7	25.5	212	New Zealand
-424	39	274	1.2	2 083	58.5	20.9	..	North Macedonia

Economy	Merchandise trade			Trade in services		GDP	
	Exports	Imports	Terms of trade	Exports	Imports	Per capita (nominal)	Growth (real)[a]
	(Millions of US$)	(Millions of US$)	(2015=100)	(Millions of US$)	(Millions of US$)	(US$)	(Percentage)
Norway	84 459	80 447	72	35 543	36 968	66 420	-0.8
Poland	271 059	257 177	101	67 007	40 202	15 706	-2.7
Portugal	61 531	77 600	99	25 570	15 744	22 647	-7.6
Romania	70 721	92 124	100	27 088	16 340	12 875	-3.9
Russian Federation	332 227	240 380	89	(e) 47 453	(e) 64 634	10 175	-3.0
Saint Pierre and Miquelon	5	99	96	-	-	..	..
San Marino	..	..	..	..	..	44 833	-8.0
Serbia	19 498	26 233	101	8 195	6 513	6 919	-2.1
Slovakia	86 104	84 464	104	10 121	8 903	19 157	-4.8
Slovenia	44 797	42 120	104	7 848	5 582	25 445	-5.5
Spain	307 015	324 994	102	89 976	60 502	27 398	-10.8
Sweden	155 601	149 880	99	69 585	68 392	53 191	-2.8
Switzerland, Liechtenstein	319 318	291 981	108	115 006	114 029	86 705	-3.0
Ukraine	49 220	53 929	106	15 509	11 074	3 477	-4.0
United Kingdom	404 681	634 742	83	342 439	204 748	39 712	-9.8
United States of America	1 431 610	2 407 527	100	705 643	460 301	63 000	-3.5
Developing economies	8 091 539	7 509 372	100	1 406 239	1 642 343	5 290	-1.8
Developing economies: Africa	386 402	508 986	99	82 682	142 816	1 863	-3.4
Algeria	21 617	35 122	70	(e) 3 200	(e) 8 003	3 233	-7.7
Angola	20 937	9 543	80	66	5 580	1 798	-4.2
Benin	2 316	3 263	101	(e) 424	(e) 580	1 277	3.8
Botswana	4 262	6 516	94	(e) 509	(e) 726	6 783	-8.0
Burkina Faso	4 372	4 117	137	(e) 453	(e) 1 578	809	1.6
Burundi	162	909	120	-	-	252	-2.5
Cabo Verde	53	720	103	290	218	3 119	-14.8
Cameroon	(e) 3 385	(e) 5 364	91	(e) 1 628	(e) 2 283	1 520	0.7
Central African Republic	(e) 125	(e) 602	95	-	-	479	0.3
Chad	(e) 2 623	(e) 2 675	79	(e) 229	(e) 1 526	674	-0.7
Comoros	21	280	47	(e) 68	(e) 97	1 371	-1.0
Congo	(e) 3 340	(e) 1 866	97	-	-	1 822	-8.3
Congo, Dem. Rep. of the	14 122	6 663	107	144	2 691	529	-0.9
Côte d'Ivoire	11 922	(e) 10 650	93	(e) 1 054	(e) 3 187	2 314	1.8
Djibouti	(e) 2 921	(e) 3 425	99	-	-	3 264	-1.0
Egypt	26 630	59 843	103	15 053	18 199	3 501	0.5
Equatorial Guinea	(e) 3 200	(e) 1 724	75	-	-	6 842	-4.9
Eritrea	(e) 556	(e) 976	104	-	-	581	-1.8
Eswatini	(e) 1 703	(e) 1 533	93	68	197	3 487	-3.6
Ethiopia	3 258	13 115	96	4 462	5 408	812	2.3
French Southern Territories	..	..	..	..	..	..	..
Gabon	(e) 4 903	(e) 2 937	92	-	-	6 997	-2.1
Gambia	61	(e) 695	101	(e) 117	(e) 102	779	-0.9
Ghana	14 472	12 429	111	(e) 8 103	(e) 12 519	2 202	0.8
Guinea	(e) 5 595	(e) 3 374	116	(e) 40	(e) 1 011	1 044	5.2
Guinea-Bissau	198	285	108	(e) 28	(e) 149	668	-2.5

Current account balance	FDI		CPI growth	Population			Fleet size[b]	Economy
	Outflows	Inflows		Total	Share of urban	Old-age dependency ratio		
(Millions of US$)	(Millions of US$)	(Millions of US$)	(Percentage)	(Thousands)	(Percentage)	(Percentage)	(1000 of dwt)	
7 185	-1 063	-2 394	1.3	5 421	83.0	26.9	24 362	Norway
20 549	1 821	10 080	3.4	37 847	60.0	28.4	101	Poland
-2 607	2 288	6 324	-0.1	10 197	66.3	35.5	22 833	Portugal
-13 138	202	2 322	2.6	19 238	54.2	29.5	79	Romania
36 113	6 311	9 676	3.4	145 934	74.8	23.5	10 899	Russian Federation
..	..	..	..	6	90.3	..	..	Saint Pierre and Miquelon
..	..	..	0.2	34	97.5	..	..	San Marino
-2 236	192	3 830	1.7	8 737	56.4	29.1	..	Serbia
-294	233	-1 930	2.0	5 460	53.8	24.6	..	Slovakia
3 957	555	529	-0.1	2 079	55.1	32.3	2	Slovenia
9 044	21 422	8 928	-0.3	46 755	80.8	30.4	1 816	Spain
30 979	31 014	26 109	0.7	10 099	88.0	32.8	1 157	Sweden
28 094	16 768	-47 172	-0.7	8 693	73.7	29.0	929	Switzerland, Liechtenstein
5 207	82	-868	2.7	43 734	69.6	25.3	391	Ukraine
-95 421	-33 409	19 724	0.9	68 145	83.7	29.3	34 074	United Kingdom
-616 087	92 811	156 321	1.2	333 968	82.8	25.7	12 458	United States of America
437 666	385 936	670 352	5.4	6 506 424	51.6	11.3	1 675 967	Developing economies
-91 054	1 592	39 785	17.8	1 339 430	43.5	6.2	325 610	Developing economies: Africa
-18 221	16	1 125	2.4	43 851	73.7	10.8	673	Algeria
872	91	-1 866	22.3	32 866	66.8	4.3	317	Angola
-619	24	176	3.0	12 123	48.4	6.0	1	Benin
-1 620	17	80	2.0	2 352	70.9	7.3	..	Botswana
83	22	149	1.9	20 903	30.6	4.5	..	Burkina Faso
(e) -517	2	6	7.3	11 891	13.7	4.5	..	Burundi
-274	-45	73	0.6	556	66.7	7.1	46	Cabo Verde
-2 149	85	488	2.8	26 546	57.6	4.9	2 739	Cameroon
(e) -187	..	35	2.3	4 830	42.2	5.2	..	Central African Republic
(e) -806	..	558	3.5	16 426	23.5	4.9	..	Chad
-67	..	9	1.1	870	29.4	5.4	1 227	Comoros
(e) -223	27	4 016	2.4	5 518	67.8	4.9	6	Congo
-1 095	149	1 647	11.3	89 561	45.6	5.9	33	Congo, Dem. Rep. of the
(e) -4 373	158	509	2.5	26 378	51.7	5.2	3	Côte d'Ivoire
366	..	240	2.9	988	78.1	7.1	1 896	Djibouti
-14 236	327	5 852	5.7	102 334	42.8	8.8	1 745	Egypt
(e) -231	..	530	4.8	1 403	73.1	3.9	53	Equatorial Guinea
(e) -156	..	74	4.9	3 546	41.3	8.3	14	Eritrea
255	-14	41	3.9	1 160	24.2	6.9	..	Eswatini
-2 719	..	2 395	20.4	114 964	21.7	6.3	338	Ethiopia
..	..	..	..	..	..	..	0	French Southern Territories
(e) -802	..	1 717	1.3	2 226	90.1	6.0	1 131	Gabon
-87	1	46	5.9	2 417	62.6	4.7	5	Gambia
-2 134	542	1 877	9.9	31 073	57.3	5.3	42	Ghana
2 685	1	325	10.6	13 133	36.9	5.5	0	Guinea
(e) -151	0	20	1.5	1 968	44.2	5.2	2	Guinea-Bissau

Economy	Merchandise trade			Trade in services		GDP	
	Exports	Imports	Terms of trade	Exports	Imports	Per capita (nominal)	Growth (real)[a]
	(Millions of US$)	(Millions of US$)	(2015=100)	(Millions of US$)	(Millions of US$)	(US$)	(Percentage)
Kenya	6 034	15 435	97	(e) 3 659	(e) 3 573	1 836	-0.3
Lesotho	888	(e) 1 811	92	12	359	996	-5.5
Liberia	608	1 102	143	(e) 11	(e) 320	505	-3.0
Libya	(e) 7 741	(e) 13 396	66	-	-	2 083	-67.6
Madagascar	1 987	3 224	72	(e) 640	(e) 789	488	-3.8
Malawi	(e) 767	(e) 2 820	91	(e) 169	(e) 292	458	0.2
Mali	3 923	4 877	140	(e) 619	(e) 2 353	875	-2.1
Mauritania	2 830	2 745	133	(e) 183	(e) 845	1 678	-2.9
Mauritius	1 791	4 234	104	(e) 1 300	(e) 1 312	9 289	-11.0
Morocco	27 159	43 831	96	13 855	7 088	3 080	-7.0
Mozambique	(e) 3 589	(e) 6 471	98	764	2 497	455	-0.5
Namibia	5 600	6 823	106	393	472	4 132	-6.5
Niger	998	2 378	96	(e) 227	(e) 1 165	566	1.2
Nigeria	35 634	55 390	81	3 993	19 833	2 082	-1.9
Rwanda	1 408	2 542	116	(e) 560	(e) 597	824	-0.2
Saint Helena	(e) 70	(e) 32	113	..	..	..	..
Sao Tome and Principe	14	(e) 136	71	35	43	1 907	-6.5
Senegal	3 929	7 812	106	(e) 887	(e) 2 396	1 496	1.9
Seychelles	432	1 004	97	670	492	11 986	-15.9
Sierra Leone	(e) 368	(e) 1 257	111	-	-	528	-2.2
Somalia	(e) 360	(e) 1 170	106	-	-	(u) 100	-3.7
South Africa	85 834	(e) 84 063	118	7 528	9 856	5 093	-7.0
South Sudan	(e) 636	(e) 988	..	(e) 99	(e) 1 122	455	-7.2
Sudan	3 803	9 838	116	(e) 1 230	(e) 1 322	1 721	-3.3
Tanzania, United Republic of	6 061	7 889	125	(e) 2 290	(e) 1 209	1 164	7.0
Togo	1 008	2 166	105	(e) 477	(e) 408	910	0.7
Tunisia	13 813	18 351	99	(e) 2 275	(e) 2 367	3 323	-8.6
Uganda	4 149	8 251	108	(e) 1 114	(e) 3 042	728	-1.7
Western Sahara	..	..	..	..	..	..	..
Zambia	7 819	5 323	102	554	1 188	1 005	-2.8
Zimbabwe	4 396	5 002	109	(e) 167	(e) 483	9 590	-9.0
Developing economies: America	954 672	917 495	104	123 796	155 076	6 845	-7.3
Anguilla	(e) 11	(e) 210	97	(e) 137	(e) 68	20 438	-18.0
Antigua and Barbuda	22	494	94	(e) 580	(e) 272	14 016	-18.3
Argentina	54 884	42 354	104	9 403	11 770	8 690	-9.9
Aruba	98	865	108	1 353	806	21 302	-30.0
Bahamas	354	1 937	97	1 288	1 414	29 216	-14.5
Barbados	345	1 518	100	(e) 787	(e) 277	15 191	-17.6
Belize	287	787	105	427	170	3 999	-15.5
Bolivia (Plurinational State of)	7 015	7 080	98	616	1 783	3 266	-10.0
Bonaire, Sint Eustatius and Saba	(e) 1	(e) 83	..	..	..	..	..
Brazil	209 878	166 276	108	28 471	49 104	6 687	-4.1
British Virgin Islands	(e) 15	(e) 190	106	-	-	36 107	-17.0
Cayman Islands	22	1 337	94	-	-	85 134	-8.0

Current account balance	FDI		CPI growth	Population			Fleet size[b]	Economy
	Outflows	Inflows		Total	Share of urban	Old-age dependency ratio		
(Millions of US$)	(Millions of US$)	(Millions of US$)	(Percentage)	(Thousands)	(Percentage)	(Percentage)	(1000 of dwt)	
-4 589	-7	717	5.3	53 771	28.0	4.3	13	Kenya
-52	..	102	4.9	2 142	29.0	7.9	..	Lesotho
..	80	87	17.0	5 058	52.1	5.9	300 088	Liberia
-	205	..	22.3	6 871	80.7	6.7	1 625	Libya
(e) -634	102	359	4.2	27 691	38.5	5.5	13	Madagascar
-1 364	7	98	8.6	19 130	17.4	4.9	..	Malawi
(e) -360	26	308	0.6	20 251	43.9	4.9	..	Mali
(e) -554	6	978	2.3	4 650	55.3	5.6	1	Mauritania
-1 374	26	246	2.5	1 272	40.8	17.7	142	Mauritius
-1 633	492	1 763	0.6	36 911	63.5	11.6	154	Morocco
-3 813	153	2 337	3.1	31 255	37.1	5.4	31	Mozambique
252	50	-75	2.6	2 541	52.0	6.0	42	Namibia
(e) -974	27	367	2.8	24 207	16.6	5.4	1	Niger
-16 976	-338	2 385	13.2	206 140	52.0	5.1	4 927	Nigeria
-1 123	..	135	8.0	12 952	17.4	5.4	..	Rwanda
..	..	..	..	6	40.1	..	..	Saint Helena
-60	1	47	9.8	219	74.4	5.4	730	Sao Tome and Principe
(e) -2 932	171	1 481	2.5	16 744	48.1	5.7	17	Senegal
-312	10	122	1.2	98	57.5	11.8	206	Seychelles
-1 001	..	349	15.7	7 977	42.9	5.2	2 848	Sierra Leone
..	..	464	..	15 893	46.1	5.7	1	Somalia
6 711	-1 973	3 106	3.3	59 309	67.4	8.4	334	South Africa
..	..	18	38.0	11 194	20.2	6.1	..	South Sudan
-5 447	..	717	163.3	43 849	35.3	6.5	6	Sudan
-1 214	..	1 013	3.0	59 734	35.2	4.9	1 730	Tanzania, United Republic of
-327	931	639	1.8	8 279	42.8	5.1	2 105	Togo
-2 512	43	652	5.7	11 819	69.6	13.3	320	Tunisia
-3 664	0	823	3.8	45 741	25.0	3.8	..	Uganda
..	..	..	..	597	86.8	4.9	..	Western Sahara
2 254	133	234	16.4	18 384	44.6	4.0	3	Zambia
-	44	194	557.2	14 863	32.2	5.5	..	Zimbabwe
-2 439	-3 542	87 574	7.7	649 923	81.0	13.3	458 234	Developing economies: America
-58	-1	26	-1.5	15	100.0	..	4	Anguilla
-109	10	22	1.1	98	24.4	13.6	6 402	Antigua and Barbuda
3 313	1 234	4 123	42.0	45 196	92.1	17.7	886	Argentina
-326	-10	114	-1.3	107	43.7	21.5	0	Aruba
-2 065	157	897	0.0	393	83.2	11.0	74 289	Bahamas
(e) -740	8	262	2.9	287	31.2	25.1	2 595	Barbados
-128	4	76	0.1	398	46.0	7.6	4 537	Belize
-176	-102	-1 048	0.9	11 673	70.1	12.0	124	Bolivia (Plurinational State of)
..	..	..	..	26	75.1	..	..	Bonaire, Sint Eustatius and Saba
-25 923	-25 808	24 778	3.2	212 559	87.1	13.8	5 218	Brazil
..	42 280	39 620	1.4	30	48.5	..	14	British Virgin Islands
(e) -661	10 835	23 621	1.0	66	100.0	..	6 725	Cayman Islands

Economy	Merchandise trade			Trade in services		GDP	
	Exports	Imports	Terms of trade	Exports	Imports	Per capita (nominal)	Growth (real)[a]
	(Millions of US$)	(Millions of US$)	(2015=100)	(Millions of US$)	(Millions of US$)	(US$)	(Percentage)
Chile	73 485	59 226	120	6 318	11 316	13 360	-5.8
Colombia	31 008	43 489	105	(e) 5 107	(e) 9 199	5 342	-6.8
Costa Rica	12 174	14 942	101	(e) 6 839	(e) 3 429	11 689	-4.5
Cuba	(e) 2 200	(e) 8 165	102	-	-	8 940	-10.8
Curaçao	271	1 210	96	(e) 760	(e) 521	18 658	-3.4
Dominica	14	213	107	(e) 68	(e) 109	6 824	-15.4
Dominican Republic	10 297	17 047	110	4 147	3 142	7 253	-6.7
Ecuador	20 227	17 959	96	1 767	2 760	5 427	-7.8
El Salvador	5 044	10 327	104	2 132	1 453	3 793	-8.6
Falkland Islands (Malvinas)	(e) 383	(e) 121	107	..	..	..	..
Grenada	22	393	84	(e) 251	(e) 167	9 360	-12.6
Guatemala	11 521	18 205	137	2 604	2 854	4 258	-2.5
Guyana	2 587	2 073	132	(e) 260	(e) 1 238	7 311	43.0
Haiti	721	2 971	101	(e) 217	(e) 568	792	-3.8
Honduras	7 683	10 241	132	1 994	1 847	2 397	-9.0
Jamaica	1 219	4 712	96	2 146	1 739	4 692	-10.1
Mexico	417 670	393 248	97	(e) 16 974	(e) 25 288	8 265	-8.2
Montserrat	6	31	102	(e) 9	(e) 13	12 017	-9.0
Nicaragua	5 087	6 545	135	943	615	1 853	-2.0
Panama	9 483	14 740	105	8 555	3 070	12 276	-17.9
Paraguay	8 529	10 217	99	846	904	5 037	-0.6
Peru	42 411	36 129	114	(e) 3 314	(e) 7 446	6 080	-11.1
Saint Barthélemy	..	..	..	..	..	..	..
Saint Kitts and Nevis	52	271	95	(e) 268	(e) 192	16 502	-15.1
Saint Lucia	55	505	99	(e) 401	(e) 207	8 335	-26.6
Saint Martin (French part)	..	..	..	..	..	..	..
Saint Vincent and the Grenadines	54	310	98	(e) 118	(e) 91	6 998	-5.5
Sint Maarten (Dutch part)	134	595	..	(e) 469	(e) 155	-	5.0
Suriname	2 345	1 329	143	103	563	5 895	-10.1
Trinidad and Tobago	(e) 5 216	(e) 4 671	92	(e) 497	(e) 1 444	15 557	-6.8
Turks and Caicos Islands	(e) 3	(e) 325	98	(e) 347	(e) 53	26 866	-15.0
Uruguay	6 857	7 564	108	3 553	3 477	13 822	-5.9
Venezuela (Bolivarian Rep. of)	(e) 4 980	(e) 6 590	66	-	-	(u) 3 573	-25.0
Developing economies: Asia and Oceania	6 750 465	6 082 891	99	1 199 760	1 344 451	6 082	-0.5
Afghanistan	(e) 732	(e) 7 171	119	700	1 105	(e) 461	-6.5
American Samoa	(e) 491	(e) 600	105	-	-	..	..
Armenia	2 544	4 559	120	1 110	963	4 275	-7.4
Azerbaijan	13 470	10 731	80	2 621	5 461	4 202	-4.3
Bahrain	14 066	12 683	98	(e) 11 468	(e) 9 263	19 955	-5.5
Bangladesh	33 605	52 804	99	6 309	8 406	1 957	2.3
Bhutan	651	899	106	135	226	3 306	0.6
Brunei Darussalam	6 608	5 342	71	351	1 206	27 466	1.2
Cambodia	(e) 17 215	(e) 19 131	98	1 945	2 068	1 605	-2.0
China	2 590 221	2 057 217	99	280 629	381 088	10 238	2.3

| Current account balance | FDI | | CPI growth | Population | | | Fleet size[b] | Economy |
	Outflows	Inflows		Total	Share of urban	Old-age dependency ratio		
(Millions of US$)	(Millions of US$)	(Millions of US$)	(Percentage)	(Thousands)	(Percentage)	(Percentage)	(1000 of dwt)	
3 370	11 583	8 386	3.0	19 116	87.7	17.9	1 010	Chile
-9 326	1 966	7 690	2.5	50 883	81.4	13.2	90	Colombia
-1 349	87	1 711	0.7	5 094	80.8	14.9	3	Costa Rica
-	..	..	7.7	11 327	77.2	23.3	354	Cuba
-689	4	164	2.2	164	89.1	27.5	1 414	Curaçao
-139	0	25	-0.3	72	71.1	..	682	Dominica
-1 541	..	2 554	3.8	10 848	82.5	11.6	68	Dominican Republic
2 469	..	1 017	-0.3	17 643	64.2	11.7	307	Ecuador
121	-1	200	0.2	6 486	73.4	13.4	0	El Salvador
..	..	..	..	3	78.5	..	3	Falkland Islands (Malvinas)
-175	0	146	-0.7	113	36.5	14.7	1	Grenada
4 249	211	915	2.4	17 916	51.8	8.2	2	Guatemala
(e) -1 295	14	1 834	0.7	787	26.8	10.7	51	Guyana
(e) -57	..	30	22.9	11 403	57.1	8.3	1	Haiti
700	47	419	3.5	9 905	58.4	7.7	803	Honduras
-18	4	366	5.2	2 961	56.3	13.4	119	Jamaica
25 953	6 528	29 079	3.4	128 933	80.7	11.4	2 137	Mexico
7	..	0	-1.9	5	9.1	..	..	Montserrat
958	40	182	3.7	6 625	59.0	8.8	3	Nicaragua
1 233	39	589	-1.6	4 315	68.4	13.1	344 200	Panama
887	..	568	1.8	7 133	62.2	10.6	103	Paraguay
(e) 1 504	503	982	1.8	32 972	78.3	13.1	446	Peru
..	..	..	..	10	(e) 72.2	..	..	Saint Barthélemy
(e) -88	-6	47	-0.6	53	30.8	..	1 375	Saint Kitts and Nevis
-219	-39	15	-1.8	184	18.8	14.4	..	Saint Lucia
..	..	..	..	39	(e) 72.2	..	..	Saint Martin (French part)
-142	-3	73	-0.6	111	53.0	14.5	2 747	Saint Vincent and the Grenadines
-286	4	25	..	43	100.0	..	..	Sint Maarten (Dutch part)
259	..	-27	34.9	587	66.1	10.8	7	Suriname
13	172	-439	0.6	1 399	53.2	16.8	28	Trinidad and Tobago
..	..	30	2.2	39	93.6	..	1	Turks and Caicos Islands
-375	17	2 630	9.8	3 474	95.5	23.4	62	Uruguay
-	-79	959	2 355.1	28 436	88.3	12.3	1 424	Venezuela (Bolivarian Rep. of)
531 159	387 886	542 992	3.7	4 517 071	49.8	12.2	892 123	Developing economies: Asia and Oceania
-3 137	37	13	5.6	38 928	26.0	4.8	..	Afghanistan
..	..	..	..	55	87.2	..	..	American Samoa
-479	-27	117	1.2	2 963	63.3	17.5	..	Armenia
-228	825	507	2.8	10 139	56.4	9.7	, 732	Azerbaijan
(e) -3 245	-205	1 007	-2.3	1 702	89.5	3.4	303	Bahrain
1 082	12	2 564	5.6	164 689	38.2	7.7	3 548	Bangladesh
-381	..	3	4.1	772	42.3	9.0	..	Bhutan
514	..	577	1.9	437	78.3	7.7	468	Brunei Darussalam
-3 076	127	3 625	2.9	16 719	24.2	7.6	431	Cambodia
273 980	132 940	149 342	2.4	1 439 324	61.4	17.0	107 647	China

Economy	Merchandise trade			Trade in services		GDP	
	Exports	Imports	Terms of trade	Exports	Imports	Per capita (nominal)	Growth (real)[a]
	(Millions of US$)	(Millions of US$)	(2015=100)	(Millions of US$)	(Millions of US$)	(US$)	(Percentage)
China, Hong Kong SAR	548 773	569 769	101	63 790	51 022	46 634	-6.1
China, Macao SAR	1 353	11 586	97	(e) 10 607	(e) 3 201	37 101	-55.7
China, Taiwan Province of	347 193	288 053	95	41 170	37 855	27 998	3.1
Cook Islands	20	105	104	-	-	21 884	2.0
Fiji	828	1 732	101	414	493	5 070	-14.9
French Polynesia	108	1 701	93	-	-	21 197	-3.0
Georgia	3 343	8 053	109	1 586	1 456	4 000	-6.2
Guam	36	(e) 600	123	-	-	..	..
India	276 302	372 854	101	203 253	(e) 153 925	1 942	-6.8
Indonesia	163 306	141 622	98	14 907	24 502	3 868	-2.1
Iran (Islamic Republic of)	53 543	38 757	95	(e) 4 625	(e) 7 138	9 048	-5.9
Iraq	(e) 41 738	(e) 44 484	79	3 803	13 796	4 313	-11.2
Jordan	7 943	17 011	96	(e) 2 459	(e) 3 010	4 272	-1.6
Kazakhstan	46 447	37 222	90	5 032	8 096	8 776	-2.6
Kiribati	9	133	103	(e) 18	(e) 70	1 636	-1.1
Korea, Dem. People's Rep. of	(e) 110	(e) 860	108	-	-	-	-4.3
Korea, Republic of	512 498	467 633	95	(e) 87 274	(e) 102 936	31 799	-1.0
Kuwait	40 116	27 738	87	(e) 7 255	(e) 18 992	25 979	-5.6
Kyrgyzstan	2 006	3 688	130	(e) 440	(e) 572	1 132	-8.6
Lao People's Dem. Rep.	6 115	5 370	110	(e) 347	(e) 445	2 650	0.5
Lebanon	4 085	11 355	115	(e) 5 006	(e) 5 746	8 655	-31.2
Malaysia	234 127	189 856	99	21 859	33 283	10 402	-5.6
Maldives	286	1 839	104	1 522	720	7 293	-29.0
Marshall Islands	(e) 44	(e) 75	104	-	-	4 055	0.0
Micronesia (Federated States of)	(e) 50	(e) 206	109	(e) 44	(e) 67	3 583	-1.0
Mongolia	7 576	5 294	115	655	2 105	3 965	-5.4
Myanmar	16 692	17 947	88	(e) 4 428	(e) 3 463	1 693	3.0
Nauru	(e) 60	(e) 43	89	-	-	12 403	0.0
Nepal	856	9 856	104	904	1 096	956	-8.5
New Caledonia	1 665	2 593	113	-	-	33 474	-4.7
Niue	1	12	91	-	-	..	..
Northern Mariana Islands	(e) 3	(e) 388	113	-	-	..	..
Oman	(e) 31 685	(e) 20 960	70	(e) 1 830	(e) 5 539	12 436	-5.9
Pakistan	21 961	45 804	114	5 353	7 543	1 158	-2.7
Palau	(e) 3	(e) 167	103	(e) 58	(e) 37	15 655	0.0
Papua New Guinea	9 229	2 642	101	(e) 181	(e) 1 322	2 658	-3.6
Philippines	63 767	90 654	100	31 410	18 331	3 153	-9.5
Qatar	51 504	25 835	65	19 429	34 698	52 211	-3.9
Samoa	37	312	102	(e) 214	(e) 112	4 012	-5.5
Saudi Arabia	173 854	137 998	94	10 248	53 883	20 159	-4.1
Singapore	362 534	329 830	91	187 564	172 689	57 754	-5.4
Solomon Islands	366	(e) 477	96	50	152	1 870	-4.5
Sri Lanka	10 047	16 055	106	(e) 3 035	(e) 3 984	3 767	-3.6
State of Palestine	(e) 2 231	(e) 7 444	98	(e) 614	(e) 1 493	2 940	-10.5

Current account balance	FDI		CPI growth	Population			Fleet size[b]	Economy
	Outflows	Inflows		Total	Share of urban	Old-age dependency ratio		
(Millions of US$)	(Millions of US$)	(Millions of US$)	(Percentage)	(Thousands)	(Percentage)	(Percentage)	(1000 of dwt)	
22 666	102 224	119 229	0.3	7 497	100.0	26.3	205 092	China, Hong Kong SAR
-	510	3 514	0.8	649	100.0	16.2	2	China, Macao SAR
94 836	14 268	8 802	-0.2	23 817	78.9	22.2	7 136	China, Taiwan Province of
..	0	7	1.0	18	75.5	..	2 928	Cook Islands
-563	14	241	-2.6	896	57.2	8.9	72	Fiji
..	-2	56	-0.1	281	62.0	13.2	22	French Polynesia
-1 988	23	617	5.2	3 989	59.5	23.6	58	Georgia
..	..	..	..	169	94.9	16.1	0	Guam
32 730	11 560	64 062	6.2	1 380 004	34.9	9.8	17 054	India
-4 452	4 467	18 581	2.0	273 524	56.6	9.2	28 750	Indonesia
-	78	1 342	36.5	83 993	75.9	9.6	20 417	Iran (Islamic Republic of)
-6 197	149	-2 896	0.6	40 223	70.9	5.9	97	Iraq
-3 080	26	726	0.4	10 203	91.4	6.3	91	Jordan
-6 273	-2 028	3 877	6.8	18 777	57.7	12.6	139	Kazakhstan
(e) 14	0	0	2.5	119	55.6	7.0	356	Kiribati
..	..	6	..		62.4	13.2	1 051	Korea, Dem. People's Rep. of
75 276	32 480	9 224	0.5	51 269	81.4	22.0	15 723	Korea, Republic of
33 500	2 427	-319	2.1	4 271	100.0	4.0	4 521	Kuwait
(e) -32	2	-331	6.3	6 524	36.9	7.5	..	Kyrgyzstan
-115	..	968	5.1	7 276	36.3	6.7	2	Lao People's Dem. Rep.
(e) -8 300	28	3 067	88.2	6 825	88.9	11.2	182	Lebanon
14 342	2 827	3 483	-1.1	32 366	77.2	10.4	10 231	Malaysia
-1 119	..	348	-1.6	541	40.7	4.7	59	Maldives
(e) 5	..	7	0.6	59	77.8	..	274 041	Marshall Islands
12	..	..	0.5	115	22.9	6.8	70	Micronesia (Federated States of)
-675	26	1 719	3.7	3 278	68.7	6.7	794	Mongolia
(e) -1 690	..	1 834	5.7	54 410	31.1	9.1	171	Myanmar
..	..	..	0.9	11	100.0	..	9	Nauru
-65	..	126	6.1	29 137	20.6	8.9	..	Nepal
..	86	443	-0.5	285	71.5	14.2	14	New Caledonia
..	..	..	..	2	46.2	..	250	Niue
..	..	..	..	58	91.8	..	..	Northern Mariana Islands
(e) -8 661	1 255	4 093	-0.9	5 107	86.3	3.3	19	Oman
245	34	2 105	10.7	220 892	37.2	7.1	868	Pakistan
(e) -83	..	24	0.0	18	81.0	..	2 189	Palau
(e) 4 635	114	-935	5.0	8 947	13.3	5.8	202	Papua New Guinea
12 979	3 525	6 542	2.6	109 581	47.4	8.6	6 240	Philippines
-3 617	2 730	-2 434	-2.7	2 881	99.2	2.0	1 148	Qatar
0	5	-1	1.5	198	17.9	8.8	603	Samoa
-19 647	4 854	5 486	3.4	34 814	84.3	4.9	13 662	Saudi Arabia
59 786	32 375	90 562	-0.2	5 850	100.0	18.0	136 400	Singapore
-25	3	9	3.4	687	24.7	6.5	7	Solomon Islands
-1 083	15	434	4.6	21 413	18.7	17.3	322	Sri Lanka
(e) -1 557	61	52	-0.7	5 101	76.7	5.5	..	State of Palestine

Economy	Merchandise trade			Trade in services		GDP	
	Exports	Imports	Terms of trade	Exports	Imports	Per capita (nominal)	Growth (real)[a]
	(Millions of US$)	(Millions of US$)	(2015=100)	(Millions of US$)	(Millions of US$)	(US$)	(Percentage)
Syrian Arab Republic	868	5 418	95	-	-	(u) 1 075	-11.7
Tajikistan	1 407	3 151	111	139	410	849	3.0
Thailand	231 468	206 992	102	31 703	46 858	7 159	-6.1
Timor-Leste	264	625	..	46	320	1 443	-6.8
Tokelau	(e) 0	(e) 0	92	..	..	..	..
Tonga	15	229	108	75	95	4 714	-1.8
Turkey	169 651	219 515	100	34 875	25 721	8 523	1.6
Turkmenistan	6 385	3 127	51	-	-	8 806	5.9
Tuvalu	0	34	-	(e) 7	(e) 25	3 919	-3.0
United Arab Emirates	(e) 319 278	(e) 225 741	98	62 138	59 523	36 100	-5.2
Uzbekistan	13 097	19 932	108	1 700	3 511	1 729	1.6
Vanuatu	46	301	107	(e) 132	(e) 146	2 749	-8.0
Viet Nam	282 725	262 620	104	(e) 18 750	(e) 17 046	2 763	2.9
Wallis and Futuna Islands	(e) 0	(e) 58	103	..	..	..	..
Yemen	(e) 1 204	(e) 7 399	90	-	-	988	-5.2
Selected groups							
Developing economies excluding China	5 501 318	5 452 155	100	1 125 610	1 261 255	3 884	-4.6
Developing economies excluding LDCs	7 910 697	7 261 832	100	1 373 269	1 581 806	6 105	-1.8
LDCs	180 843	247 539	105	32 970	60 537	1 092	0.0
LLDCs	167 441	205 881	99	29 506	53 669	1 733	-2.0
SIDS (UN-OHRLLS)	419 032	416 929	93	230 509	205 822	10 630	-6.9
HIPCs (IMF)	129 256	161 361	111	30 946	58 712	976	0.1
BRICS	3 494 462	2 920 790	100	567 334	658 607	6 371	0.0
G20	13 566 119	13 766 169	100	4 013 655	3 659 377	14 932	-3.4

[a] In constant 2015 United States dollars.
[b] As of 1 January 2021.

Current account balance	FDI		CPI growth	Population			Fleet size[b]	Economy
	Outflows	Inflows		Total	Share of urban	Old-age dependency ratio		
(Millions of US$)	(Millions of US$)	(Millions of US$)	(Percentage)	(Thousands)	(Percentage)	(Percentage)	(1000 of dwt)	
(e) -2 606	..	..	113.6	17 501	55.5	7.6	78	Syrian Arab Republic
336	70	107	8.6	9 538	27.5	5.3	..	Tajikistan
17 597	16 716	-6 100	-0.8	69 800	51.4	18.4	6 059	Thailand
-357	694	72	0.5	1 318	31.3	7.3	0	Timor-Leste
..	..	..	..	1	0.0	..	..	Tokelau
-19	0	0	0.2	106	23.1	10.0	37	Tonga
-37 304	3 240	7 880	12.3	84 339	76.1	13.4	6 425	Turkey
(e) -3 577	..	1 169	7.6	6 031	52.5	7.4	125	Turkmenistan
(e) 11	..	0	1.6	12	64.0	..	1 994	Tuvalu
(e) 10 973	18 937	19 884	-2.1	9 890	87.0	1.5	753	United Arab Emirates
-3 007	2	1 726	12.9	33 469	50.4	7.2	..	Uzbekistan
28	2	30	2.9	307	25.5	6.2	1 820	Vanuatu
12 487	380	15 800	3.2	97 339	37.3	11.4	10 269	Viet Nam
..	..	..	..	11	0.0	..	2	Wallis and Futuna Islands
(e) -1 219	..	..	26.2	29 826	37.9	5.0	443	Yemen
								Selected groups
163 685	252 996	521 010	7.4	5 067 100	48.8	9.5	1 568 320	Developing economies excluding China
470 342	383 135	646 742	4.8	5 449 293	54.9	12.1	1 357 607	Developing economies excluding LDCs
-32 676	2 801	23 610	22.4	1 057 131	34.6	6.2	318 360	LDCs
-29 396	-903	15 392	20.3	533 143	31.3	6.6	2 894	LLDCs
49 142	33 614	96 894	2.1	68 287	60.9	12.7	533 194	SIDS (UN-OHRLLS)
-31 130	2 684	22 938	7.2	760 191	36.8	5.5	312 947	HIPCs (IMF)
323 611	123 030	250 964	3.1	3 237 131	52.5	13.9	141 152	BRICS
283 456	500 487	658 795	2.1	4 894 252	60.8	17.1	614 583	G20

6.2 Classifications

Classification of economies

There is no established convention for the designation of "developing" and "developed" countries or areas in the United Nations system. The designation of economies used in this handbook follows, contrary to previous editions, the differentiation between developing and developed regions made in the "Standard Country or Area Codes for Statistical Use (M49)", known as M49 (UNSD, 2020). The category "transition economies" is no longer used. The figures presented for these groups are therefore not comparable with the figures from previous editions of the handbook. For further details on UNCTAD's new development classification scheme, see UNCTAD (2021e). For a comparison of M49 with the previous UNCTAD development status classification, and with classification schemes used by other international organisations, see Hoffmeister (2020).

Throughout the handbook, the group of developing economies is further broken down into the following three regions: "Africa", "America", "Asia and Oceania", where the group of African developing economies coincides with Africa, and the group of American developing economies coincides with Latin America and the Caribbean, as defined in the "Standard Country or Area Codes for Statistical Use (M49)" (UNSD, 2020). Apart from these five groups of economies, whenever possible, data are also presented for the following groups:

- Developing economies excluding China,

- Developing economies excluding LDCs,

- LDCs, according to the UN-OHRLLS (2021),

- LLDCs, according to the UN-OHRLLS (ibid.),

- SIDS according to the UN-OHRLLS (ibid.),

- HIPCs, according to the IMF (2021),

- Brazil, Russia, India, China and South Africa (BRICS),

- Group of Twenty (G20) (Italy, 2021).

The present handbook edition now applies a broader list of SIDS maintained by UN-OHRLLS. For a discussion of the different groupings of SIDS in use, see MacFeely et al. (2021).

The UNCTADstat classification page (UNCTAD, 2021e) provides the lists of the economies included in the different groups.

Classification of goods

For breakdowns of international merchandise trade by *product*, UNCTADstat applies SITC, Revision 3, (UNSD, 1991) and various aggregates compiled on the basis of that classification. In chapter 1 of this handbook, reference is made to the following five product groups:

- All food items (SITC codes 0, 1, 22 and 4),

- Agricultural raw materials (SITC code 2 except 22, 27 and 28),

- Ores, metals, precious stones and non-monetary gold (SITC codes 27, 28, 68, 667 and 971),

- Fuels (SITC code 3),

- Manufactured goods (SITC codes 5, 6, 7 and 8 except 667 and 68).

For the measurement of movements in *commodity* prices in section 4.1, the UCPI is disaggregated by commodity groups constructed from HS 2007 (World Customs Organization, 2006). For the correspondence between these commodity groups and HS headings and for the individual price quotations represented therein, see UNCTAD (2018).

Classification of services

The breakdown by service category in section 2.2 is based on EBOPS 2010 (United Nations et al., 2012). The EBOPS 2010 main categories have been grouped as shown in table 6.2 below.

Table 6.2 | Grouping of service categories on the basis of EBOPS 2010

EBOPS 2010	Section 2.2
Transport	Transport
Travel	Travel
Insurance and pension services	Insurance, financial, intellectual property, and other business services
Financial services	
Charges for the use of intellectual property n.i.e.	
Other business services	
Telecommunications, computer and information services	Telecommunications, computer and information
Personal, cultural and recreational services	Other categories
Government goods and services n.i.e.	
Construction	
Services not allocated	
Manufacturing services on physical inputs owned by others	
Maintenance and repair services n.i.e.	

Classification of economic activities

In section 3.1, gross value added is broken down by the three broad groups of economic activities below, in accordance with the International Standard Industrial Classification of All Economic Activities (ISIC), Revision 3 (UNSD, 1989):

- Agriculture, comprising: agriculture, hunting, forestry and fishing (ISIC divisions 01 to 05),

- Industry, comprising: mining and quarrying, manufacturing, electricity, gas and water supply, construction (ISIC divisions 10 to 45),

- Services, comprising all other economic activities (ISIC divisions 50 to 99).

6.3 Calculation methods

The **annual average growth rate** over multiple years is calculated in this handbook as least squares growth rate or as exponential growth rate.

The **least squares growth rate** is computed as the coefficient b when fitting the regression model

$$\ln(y_{t+i}) = a + bi \quad \text{for } i \in \{0, 1, 2, ..., k\}$$

with least squares, where k stands for the length of the time period (in years), t for the base year, and y represents the object of measurement. This method takes all observations in the analyzed period into account.

The **exponential growth rate** is calculated as $\quad b = \frac{1}{k} \ln\left(\frac{y_{t+k}}{y_t}\right)$

Throughout the handbook, the growth rates of monetary values are based on current prices, unless otherwise specified.

The **trade openness index** (map 1.4) is calculated as the ratio of the arithmetic mean of merchandise exports (x) and imports (m) to GDP (y):

$$TOI_{i,t} = \frac{\frac{1}{2}(x_{i,t} + m_{i,t})}{y_{i,t}}$$

where i designates the economy and t the year.

The **terms of trade index** (figure 1.4.1, tables 1.4.1 and 1.4.2) with base year 2015 is calculated as follows:

$$ToT_{i,t} = 100 \frac{\frac{UVI_{exports,i,t}}{UVI_{imports,i,t}}}{\frac{UVI_{exports,i,2015}}{UVI_{imports,i,2015}}}$$

where $UVI_{exports,i,t}$ is the unit value index of exports and $UVI_{imports,i,t}$ the unit value index of imports of economy i at time t.

The **market concentration index of exports** (figure 1.4.2) is calculated as a normalized Herfindahl-Hirschmann index:

$$MCI_{exports,i} = \frac{\sqrt{\sum_{j=1}^{n} \left(\frac{x_{i,j}}{X_i}\right)^2} - \sqrt{\frac{1}{n}}}{1 - \sqrt{\frac{1}{n}}}, \text{ with } X_i = \sum_{j=1}^{n} x_{i,j}$$

where $x_{i,j}$ is the value of exports of product i from economy j and n is the number of economies.

The **volume index of exports (imports)** (figure 1.4.3, tables 1.4.1 and 1.4.2) is calculated by dividing the export (import) value index by the corresponding unit value index and scaling up by 100:

$$QI_{i,t} = 100 \frac{VI_{i,t}}{UVI_{i,t}}$$

where $VI_{i,t}$ is the value index of exports (imports), given by

$$VI_{i,t} = 100 \frac{x_{i,t}}{x_{i,2015}}$$

$x_{i,t}$ is the value of exports (imports), $UVI_{i,t}$ is the unit value index of exports (imports), i designates the economy and t the time period.

The **purchasing power index of exports** (table 1.4.1 and 1.4.2) is calculated by dividing the export value index by the corresponding import unit value index and scaling up by 100:

$$PPI_{exports,i,t} = 100 \frac{VI_{exports,i,t}}{UVI_{imports,i,t}}$$

where $VI_{exports,i,t}$ is the value index of exports (as defined above), $UVI_{imports,i,t}$ is the unit value index of imports, i designates the economy and t the time period.

The **Lorenz curve** in figure 3.1.3 plots cumulative population shares ordered by GDP per capita, on the x-axis, against the cumulative shares of global GDP which they account for, on the y-axis. For the construction of the Lorenz curve, the n economies of the world are ordered with reference to their GDP per capita, so that

$$\frac{y_i}{p_i} \geq \frac{y_{i-1}}{p_{i-1}} \text{ for all } i \in \{2, 3, ..., n\}$$

where y_i is GDP and p_i the population of the economy at position i in this ranking, counted from below.

The cumulative population shares, measured on the x-axis, are calculated as

$$P_i = \sum_{j=1}^{i} \frac{p_j}{p} \quad \text{with } p = p_1 + p_2 + ... + p_n$$

The cumulative shares of global GDP, measured on the y-axis, are calculated as follows:

$$Y_i = \sum_{j=1}^{i} \frac{y_j}{y} \quad \text{with } y = y_1 + y_2 + ... + y_n$$

The **UNCTAD Commodity Price Index** (section 3.4) is a fixed base-weight Laspeyres index with base year 2015=100. It is calculated as

$$L_t = \frac{\sum_{i=1}^{n} p_{i,t}\, q_{i,2015}}{\sum_{i=1}^{n} p_{i,2015}\, q_{i,2015}}$$

where i is the identifier of the commodity group, $q_{i,2015}$ is the quantity in which products of commodity group i were exported by developing economies during the three years around the base year (from 2014 to 2016), and $p_{i,t}$ is the price of a representative product, within commodity group i, in year t. For more details, see UNCTAD (2018).

The **nowcasts** of world merchandise exports (section 1.1) and world services exports (section 2.1) represent real-time evaluations of these variables based on a large set of relevant and timely indicators. They are based on dynamic factor models which capture common latent trends in these data through their cross correlations. In their state-space representation, the models can be written as:

$$G_t = Bh_t + u_t$$
$$h_t = Dh_{t-1} + v_t$$

where G_t is a combination of the reference and indicator series, h_t is the time-varying factor, B is a matrix of factor loadings, D defines the time structure of the respective factor, and the error terms u_t and v_t are independently distributed according to distributions N(0,W) and N(0,Q), respectively. The nowcast for the target variable at time t is obtained by extracting the corresponding element from vector G_t above, once B and the latent factor h_t have been estimated through maximum likelihood. This model is adapted to accommodate variables of different frequencies and unbalanced datasets. It should be noted that the nowcast figures cannot be considered as official data, as they are the result of an estimation. For more details on the methodology, see Cantú (2018).

6.4 References

Cantú F (2018). Estimation of a coincident indicator for international trade and global economic activity. UNCTAD Research Paper No. 27. UNCTAD.

Hoffmeister O (2020). Development status as a measure of development. Available at https://unctad.org/en/PublicationsLibrary/ser-rp-2020d5_en.pdf (accessed 10 November 2021).

IMF (2009). Balance of Payment and International Investment Position Manual. Washington DC.

IMF (2021). Factsheet. Available at https://www.imf.org/en/About/Factsheets/Sheets/2016/08/01/16/11/Debt-Relief-Under-the-Heavily-Indebted-Poor-Countries-Initiative (accessed 10 November 2021).

Italy (2021). G20 Members. Available at https://g20.org (accessed 20 October 2021).

MacFeely S, Hoffmeister O, Barnat N, Hopp D and Peltola A (2021). Constructing a criteria-based classification for Small Island Developing States: an investigation. Available at https://unctad.org/webflyer/constructing-criteria-based-classification-small-island-developing-states-investigation (accessed 11 May 2021).

UN DESA (2018). World Urbanization Prospects. The 2018 Revision: Methodology. ESA/P/WP/252. New York.

UN DESA (2019a). World Population Prospects 2019: Highlights. United Nations publication. Sales No. E.19.XIII.4. New York.

UN DESA (2019b). World Population Prospects 2019: Methodology of the United Nations population estimates and projections. ST/ESA/SER.A/425. New York.

UN DESA (2019c). World Urbanization Prospects 2018: Highlights. United Nations publication. Sales No. E19.XIII.6. New York.

UN DESA (2021). United Nations expert group meeting on the impact of the COVID-19 pandemic on fertility. Population Division. Expert Group Meeting Report. ESA/P/WP/264. New York.

UNCTAD (2018). UNCTAD Commodity Price Index. Methodological Note. Commodity Price Bulletin, No. UNCTAD/STAT/CPB/MN/1.

UNCTAD (2021a). UNCTADStat. Available at https://unctadstat.unctad.org/EN/Index.html (accessed 11 January 2021).

UNCTAD (2021b). Trade and Development Report 2021. From Recovery to Resilience: The Development Dimension. United Nations publication. Sales No. E.22.II.D.1. New York and Geneva.

UNCTAD (2021c). World Investment Report 2021: Investing in Sustainable Recovery. United Nations publication. Sales No. E.21.II.D.13. New York and Geneva.

UNCTAD (2021d). Review of Maritime Transport 2021. United Nations publication. Sales No. E.21.11.D.21. New York and Geneva.

UNCTAD (2021e). UNCTADStat: Classifications. Available at https://unctadstat.unctad.org/EN/Classifications.html (accessed 10 June 2021).

UNCTAD (2021f). Global merchandise and services trade nowcast. (accessed 25 October 2021).

United Nations (2011). International Merchandise Trade Statistics: Concepts and Definitions 2010. ST/ESA/STAT/SER.M/52/Rev.3. United Nations publication. Sales No. E.10.XVII.13.

United Nations et al. (2012). Manual on Statistics of International Trade in Services 2010. United Nations publication. Sales No. E.10.XVII.14. Geneva.

United Nations (2017). Resolution adopted by the General Assembly on 6 July 2017 on the Work of the Statistical Commission pertaining to the 2030 Agenda for Sustainable Development. A/RES/71/313. New York.

United Nations (2021). UN Comtrade Database. Available at https://comtrade.un.org/ (accessed 1 January 2021).

United Nations, European Commission, IMF, OECD, and World Bank (2009). System of National Accounts 2008. United Nations publication. Sales No. E.08.XVII.29. New York.

UN-OHRLLS (2021). Office of the High Representative for the Least Developed Countries, Landlocked Developing Countries and Small Island Developing States. Available at https://www.un.org/ohrlls/ (accessed 10 November 2021).

UNSD (1989). International Standard Industrial Classification of All Economic Activities. Revision 3. Statistical papers, No. ST/ESA/STAT/SER.M/4/Rev.3. United Nations publication. Sales No. E.90.XVII.11.

UNSD (1991). Standard International Trade Classification, Rev. 3. Statistical papers, No. ST/ESA/STAT/SER.M/34/Rev.3. United Nations publication. Sales No. E.86.XVII.12.

UNSD (2020). Standard country or area codes for statistical use (M49). Available at https://unstats.un.org/unsd/methodology/m49/ (accessed 28 May 2020).

World Customs Organization (2006). Amendments to the Harmonized System Nomenclature. Effective from 1 January 2007. Brussels.